G000016301

OMNIBUS PRESS
LONDON · NEW YORK · SYDNEY

ROSES
Low life in the Fast lane
Eddy McSquare

Cover designed by Four Corners
Book designed by Liz Nicholson
and Monica Chrysostomou

ISBN 0.7119.3227.1
Order No: OP45616

Exclusive distributors:

Book Sales Limited,
8/9 Frith Street,
London W1V 5TZ, UK.

Music Sales Corporation,
225 Park Avenue South,
New York, NY 10003, USA.

Music Sales Pty Limited,
120 Rothschild Avenue,
Rosebery, NSW 2018, Australia.

To the Music Trade only:
Music Sales Limited,
8/9 Frith Street,
London W1V 5TZ, UK.

The author wishes to thank the following magazines for source material: Faces, Smash Hits, Guitar For The Practising Musician, RIP, Circus, Metallix, Rolling Stone, Hit Parader, Kerrang!, Heavy Metal Sex Stars, Sounds, Music Connection, LA Times, Rock Scene, Metal Edge and Metal Shop.

Picture supplied by All Action Pictures, Larry Busacca, Celebrity Photo, Krasner/Trebitz, London Features International (UK & USA), Barry Plummer, Relay, Retna, Jim Smeal/Ron Galella Ltd, Starfile, Michael Uhll/Ebet Roberts.

Every effort has been made to trace the copyright holders of the photographs in this book but one or two were unreachable. We would be grateful if the photographers concerned would contact us.

Typeset by The Type Bureau, London
Printed and bound
in Singapore.

NTENTS
Guns n' Roses

INTRO

"Words from the Wise Guys"

"Guns N' Roses? Yeah, they'll make it . . . if they live long enough."

Geffen Employee (Press Release)

"You are the loudest band I've ever seen in my life."

Geffen A&R Rep

"Axl was a very quiet, soft spoken guy, maybe even a little shy. I think Axl is still that way, but people around him have changed . . ."

Anon., Circus, April '89

I feel sorry for bands like Guns N' Roses . . . They went from being virtually unheard of to becoming world-wide superstars in less than a year. They've had to adjust to it very quickly and it's not at all surprising to see the sort of drug and alcohol abuse people in that sort of situation usually fall into."

Geoff Tate of Queensryche, Metallix, '89

Forged on the mean streets of Hollywood and fired to rock-hard intensity under the blazing California sun, Guns N' Roses are the sort of five-headed monster-child that only Los Angeles, America's whore of Babylon, could have spawned.

A twisted variation on American Dream/melting pot clichés, Guns N' Roses' members converged in L.A. from disparate parts of the United States and England, driven by hope and necessity and a burning case of the hots for playing rock 'n' roll. There, in a city of false faces and facades, where phoniness is a fact of life, they slowly merged and carved a notorious niche for themselves, fuelled by gritty self-confidence and a compulsion to survive.

Patched together from fragments of two local bands – Hollywood Rose and L.A. Guns–Guns N' Roses officially came into being in the early summer of '85. Their paths had crossed innumerable times on L.A.'s incestuous rock scene; but what was it that attracted these particular individuals together, and what exactly is it that constitutes their explosive interpersonal chemistry? Guns N' Roses' lead guitarist, the mystery known simply as Slash has one theory: "The way I grew up wasn't a normal, regular childhood. Everyone in this band has some quirk, our own stories and that's why we fit together so well. That has a lot to do with our sense of feeling and soul."

Left-handed bass player Duff McKagan's story begins slightly to the north of Los Angeles. Born Michael McKagan on February 5, 1964, the youngest of eight children, Duff hails originally from Seattle, Washington. He describes his home city as "a rowdy rock 'n' roll town with a hip underground". Back when Duff was just a brown-haired kid who couldn't make up his mind whether he wanted to play electric guitar or bass or drums, the Seattle music scene was thriving. "There were millions of bands and places to play," he remembers. That's barely an exaggeration: Duff passed through over 31 bands during his early days in Seattle – including a hardcore punk bank called the Fartz. While there was an overabundance of opportunities to meet other musicians and jam, playing Seattle clubs was ultimately a dead end for a serious musician. "You [wouldn't] get anywhere, except for Queensryche, who got signed; but for me, Seattle was a good training ground."

Like future bandmates Slash and Axl, Duff was totally into The Sex Pistols; in fact, Duff cites Sid Vicious as his sole musical influence because . . . he was the coolest bass player ever. Little wonder then, that upon arriving in L.A., Duff chose to devote himself entirely to bass playing. He traded all his gear for a bass and a small bass amp speculating, "There's a million guitar players down here and I wasn't that good. So just to get my foot in the door, I said, 'Okay, I'll come playing bass, because bass players are pretty rare to find.' Basically, that's how I got started. I wasn't really that good at the beginning."

Nineteen-year-old Duff McKagan, who'd earned his living as a musician for the past four years, found himself starting from scratch. He didn't know a soul in town, except for a brother who lived out in the San Fernando Valley, but he was thrilled nonetheless: "It was a good learning experience for me in a lot of ways, to move to a big city and not know anybody. It was an exciting feeling, just coming here and not knowing what the next day was going to involve."

That sense of the unexpected Duff sought caught up with him one day when he answered a local newspaper ad reading something like, "Looking for a bass player – Aerosmith, Alice Cooper. Slash." Judging by the name, Duff expected some punk with a penchant for '70s rock; but when he kept the appointed rendezvous at Canter's (L.A.'s "legendary" 24 hour deli and rock hangout) he found two long-haired guys instead. "When I met Slash and Steve [Adler] for the first time, it was weird, 'cause I'd never met guys like this before – L.A. locals. We went out that night and got drunk, and then we had this ill-fated band. It was Slash's band, Road Crew."

Contrary to Duff's initial impression, Slash isn't exactly an L.A. native, nor is he simply the perpetually inebriated, pussy-chasing, cartoonish "Cousin It" he may appear to be. A very alert and intuitive mind ticks away under that distinguished top hat. Though reticent about such pertinent details as his real name, Slash's unusual upbringing clearly had a major influence on the direction his life and career took.

English-born of an interracial couple (according to *Rolling Stone*, who care about these things), Slash came into the world on July 23, 1965 in Stoke-On-Trent. His dad, Anthony Hudson, was a successful album cover designer (among his credits are a Neil Young album and Joni Mitchell's 'Court and Spark'). Ola Hudson designed clothing for rock's glitterati, including David Bowie's outfit for *The Man Who Fell To Earth*. "My mom and dad were both in the music business very major. We used to be, like, really rich, as far as that goes . . ." Rich or not, when Slash's family moved to Los Angeles from England, the young man had to make many cultural adjustments.

"Growing up in Stoke-On-Trent was great," Slash recalls fondly, "an entirely different atmosphere, a different set of morals as far as things considered important. In Northern England, there's a difference in what's held in high regard. It's a lot tougher there; school is different. I fought a lot when I was real young; I'm usually calm now."

While Slash found British schooling a trifle on the violent side, his opinion of US educational standards was even lower: "The public school system really sucks! If there was nothing to hold my attention I was off. The older I got, the less willing I was to put up with being told what to do in school-having to do a paper or this or that. The older I got, the less I did it. And then I started playing guitar . . . that was the beginning of the end."

At the age of 14, Slash was still without a guitar; but a chance encounter in a playground with a reckless skateboarder changed his life. "I was hanging out at this elementary school because they had these [half-pipe] banks – I used to be into freestyle on bicycles – [and there was this kid who] had fallen off his skateboard. I thought he had killed himself. I went over to see if he was alright, and we started hanging out after that." The accident-prone sidewalk surfer was none other than future Guns drummer Steve "Popcorn" Adler.

Born January 22, 1965 in Cleveland, Ohio, Steve found Guns N' Roses' arduous touring lifestyle nothing new. He was unceremoniously tossed out of his home when he was only 12 years old. "A super bad guy just seemed to come out of me when I was a wee youngster," Steve explains. "I was *really* bad: got thrown out of eight, nine different schools, I used to fight with the teachers, I'd get in a fight every day . . . I was just a feisty little kid."

"Feisty" though he may have been, his mania for music manifested itself early on. Steve remembers listening to Frankie Valli and the Four Seasons back when he was just five years old. Adler's early drum role models were Roger Taylor of Queen, Gene Krupa, Led Zeppelin's John Bonham and The Who's Keith Moon. Naturally drawn to the skins, Steve never took a lesson in his life and didn't own a kit until he was 18 years old. The frustrated novice contented himself by pounding on books and Tupperware. "I learned from watching and listening very closely to other drummers. That, plus wanting it real bad and believing in myself." (METALLIX, Summer).

SAFEW

SLASH

Slash remembers the inauspicious formation of 2/5ths of G'N'R: "Steven and I went to Bancroft Junior High together that fall . . . we ended up ditching the entire seventh grade. Anyway, he had a guitar at his grandmother's place in Hollywood where he was staying. He used to play KISS songs. Actually, he couldn't play anything, but it was a huge turn on for him," as it was for Slash, who was soon logging in up to twelve hours a day on the fretboard.

Slash never really benefited from any formal music training as such; although he attended music school, the instructions he received didn't quite provide him with the ammo to achieve the sound he aimed for. "There was a teacher at school, Robert, and he started showing me the total rudiments of guitar, like 'Mary Had A Little Lamb' and all that sh*t, and that didn't sound anything like what I wanted to learn. I wanted to be playing 'Smoke On The Water' and such." Eventually Slash developed a more practical approach; Robert let him hang out and observe his technique and Slash just took it from there.

"I started from the get go. As soon as I could play a bar chord, I started playing in bands. I don't even remember a space in time when I was learning to play and not playing with somebody else. I was so focused – even in junior high – knowing that this was the only thing I ever wanted to do that I went through a lot of people because they were not willing to give up everything – school, home – just to jam. Steve is the only guy I stuck with, because he was as into it as I was."

Before long, Steve, Slash and Duff's short-lived career as Road Crew fizzled and they began searching for new outlets for their talent. Bands disintegrating, metamorphosing and re-shuffling was a way of life on LA's dog-eat-dog club circuit. Slash, who'd been active on the local scene for years, once actually auditioned for those perennial GN'R favourites, Poison. (He allegedly failed the audition because he wasn't considered pretty enough for their glam standards.)

Growing up on the fringes of the professional music business, Slash was "exposed to a lot of Hollywood bull at a very early age." He'd seen the mighty and the meek, but by his own admission, he eventually met his match: "The only thing that weirded me out about living in Hollywood was meeting a guy from Indiana." That "guy from Indiana", a wiry kid with a tinderbox temper, became Slash's most fervent ally in the war against musical mediocrity. He was known by the name of W. Axl Rose.

Born on February 6, 1962 W. Axl Rose was raised as William, or Bill, Bailey, son of L. Stephen and Sharon Bailey in Lafayette, Indiana. Axl's natural father abandoned his wife Sharon and her brood. When Sharon remarried, the children's surnames changed accordingly.

Although he considered L. Stephen Bailey his "real dad", when Axl discovered his hidden past he decided to adopt his genetic father's last name and was briefly known as W. Rose. "Axl" came from one of his old Indiana groups, and his friends suggested he incorporate it into his new moniker. Later on, Bill Bailey legally became W. Axl Rose.

VICTORY OR DEATH

The Bailey household was strictly religious. The family attended a "holy roller" Pentecostal country church. Despite his upbringing and his initial religious faith, Axl laments, ". . . Nothing ever happened to me. I watched my father speak in tongues and people interpret it. I watched him sing in perfect Japanese – and my dad doesn't know Japanese – and sing every note right on key with his eyes closed, driving 100 miles an hour down the freeway and not hitting a car. I don't know how that happened. I've seen people healed . . . I've seen people with no eyes read. It was very strange, but nothing ever happened [to me]. I always won all the Bible contests. I taught Sunday school. I played piano. I knew more gospel songs than anybody I knew." In spite of his elevated spiritual aspirations, the big pay-off somehow eluded him. "I always thought I was cursed or something. Now I just feel pissed off. If there's somebody up there, I don't know. I just don't have a clue about it."

It didn't take long for Axl's non-conformist side to emerge, albeit in a harmless fashion. As a choirboy, he confused the teacher by singing high vocal parts, though he was supposed to be second baritone. "My teacher had ears like a bat, so in order to get away with singing someone else's part, you'd really have to get it down. He used to wonder how come he's hearing a soprano in the bass section."

By Axl's own account, in high school he was "an athlete, a real jock." Nonetheless, he found himself continually warring with school authorities concerning what were, in his opinion, ridiculous, inconsequential orders and rules. After a few years, the rebel in Axl emerged in earnest; he grew his hair long, smoked pot, and decided that since he was already perpetually in the doghouse, he might as well give "them" a good reason to bust his nuts. Axl gradually bloomed into a full-fledged juvenile delinquent, and by the age of 16 was exiled from his parents' home.

"I remember when I was in junior high and they talked about finding a goal – 'Yeah, I'm gonna do this, I'm gonna do that' – all just trying to impress the teacher to get a grade. If they get a good grade, they get an allowance. I was like, 'No. I wanna be in a band and I wanna do [great things]'. So I got an 'F' for thinking grandiose thoughts."

Despite his choral training, when the idea of joining a band first struck Axl, he didn't envision himself as a vocalist. He was willing to do anything to be part of a group; he tried his hand at the keyboards and then changed over to bass. But by and by, Axl ended up "on the mike" out of necessity, because he was the only guy who could hit more than one note a week.

Before managing to escape his homestate, the aspiring singer was chucked in jail "over 20 times" by his own estimate, spending up to three months inside. Serving as his own lawyer (can you picture *that?*) 'cause I didn't trust the public defenders for *sh*t*", he admits his guilt on five of those occasions, for "public consumption" – ie, drinking while underage; the other arrests, he insists, were motivated solely by the animosity between him and local law.

Noting an above average IQ, a psychiatrist once assessed Axl's behaviour as evidence of psychosis, and *Rolling Stone Magazine* revealed that Axl has been prescribed lithium to combat a manic-depressive disorder; but Axl remains dubious about the diagnosis and treatment he's received: "I'm very sensitive and emotional and things upset me and make me feel like not functioning or dealing with people . . . I went to a clinic, thinking it would help my moods. The only thing I did was to take one 500 question test – ya know, filling in the little black dots. All of a sudden I'm diagnosed manic-depressive. 'Let's put Axl on medication.' Well, the medication doesn't help me deal with stress. The only thing it does is help keep people off my back because they figure I'm on medication."

One of excitable Axl's best teenhood buds was Jeff Isabelle, nicknamed Izzy. Like Axl, guitarist Izzy Stradlin was a Lafayette native, born April 8, 1962. Izzy remembers Axl was, "like a serious lunatic when I met him. He was just really fucking bent on fighting and destroying things. Somebody'd look at him wrong, and he'd just, like start a fight. And you think about Lafayette, man, there's like fuck all to do." As with Axl, there was no love lost between Izzy and Indiana. Guns N' Roses only high school grad, Izzy decided he'd rather run than fight (probably for the last time in his life), and after receiving his diploma in 1979, he hightailed it out of the Midwest's stagnant social cesspool, bee-lining for the glittery, beckoning Hollywood Hills.

Slash was introduced to the Indiana contingent when he responded to an ad Izzy and Axl placed in a local L.A. paper; unfortunately, Slash failed the audition. As Axl tells it, "He was too bluesy at the time and too good; we thought he was too far into what he was doing, and we wouldn't be able to relate. But little by little, we kept bumping into each other in clubs." When Izzy saw a caricature Slash had drawn of Aerosmith and asked for a copy of it, things got off on a better foot. Slash recalls: "We got to talking and he came over to my place later on and he played me this tape of his band. It had this tiny little voice shrieking in the background." That tiny voice belonged to W. Axl Rose, lead singer of Izzy's combo, Hollywood Rose. Ironically, while Slash attempted to lure Axl away from Izzy for his own devices, Axl split for another local band, guitarist Tracii Guns' group, L.A. Guns. Axl "explains" what happened next:

"I left Hollywood Rose and joined L.A. Guns and the drummer and bass player freaked out and we kinda broke up. In the meantime, Izzy had booked a gig for Hollywood Rose and there was no band left, then Tracii booked a gig for L.A. Guns and there was no band there either. We mixed what was left of the two bands and we got Guns N' Roses. Then Tracii left and went back to L.A. Guns and we got Duff. This line-up was finalized on June 6th, 1985." Slash was quickly assimilated into the new line-up, and after two days of rehearsal the final chapter of Guns N' Roses played its debut gig on a Thursday night at L.A.'s Troubadour.

Four days later, the new-found GN'R embarked on their first tour, intending to plough through Seattle, Portland, Eugene, Sacramento and San Francisco; however, their grand scheme fell to bits when their car broke down in Fresno. Guitars in hand and in full regalia, they were forced to hitchhike from Fresno straight on up the coast. After a truck driver dumped them on the highway some 20 hours north, two ex-hippy girls from Frisco picked them up. Their spirits bolstered by some herbally enhanced brownies, Guns N' Roses made it to the gig, playing with amps borrowed from the opening act. Walking away from the show with only a fifth of the $250 they'd been promised, they discovered that the rest of the tour was cancelled, and wearily thumbed it back home. With philosophical hindsight, Izzy observes, "It was like a test . . ." After that adventure, Los Angeles seemed like a walk in the park.

Upon returning, hard times continued to beleaguer the band. Success was *not* right around the corner; in fact, until they got signed, corners were literally Guns N' Roses home – unless they could arrange to crash at somebody's house. Axl floated from place to place, never spending more than two months at any location, welcoming brief sojourns in abandoned apartments. Slash reminisces, "We'd walk up and down Hollywood Boulevard and visit every porno store there is, 'cause they stay open 24 hours."

At one point all five lived together in a one room rehearsal studio on Gardener Street in L.A. Measuring a mere four feet by twelve feet, it lacked bathroom, shower and kitchen, but came with plenty of holes in the ceiling to let in the rain. "A very uncomfortable prison cell," recalls Slash. "But God, did we sound good in there! We're a really loud band and we don't compromise the volume for anything! We'd bash away with a couple of Marshalls in this tiny room, and it was cool because all the losers from Sunset and all the bands would come over and hang out there every night."

Axl adds, "Every weekend, the biggest party in L.A. was down at our place. We'd have 500 people packed in an alley and our old roadie was selling beers for a buck out of his trunk. It was like a bar and everyone had their whiskey. We could get away with whatever we wanted, except when the cops came . . . If there was a problem with someone, we'd escort them out. By 'escort' I mean we'd drag 'em out by their hair down the alley, naked."

With the entirety of Guns N' Roses living, rehearsing, wining and dining and going berserk in the same room, things became rather claustrophobic, so they pieced together a loft from some stolen wood and slept above their equipment. "The funny thing is," Axl muses, "we almost miss it . . ."

And just what did they do for money in those trying times? "G-I-R-L-S" spells Steve. Izzy elaborates: ". . . Sold drugs, sold girls, sold, uh . . . We just got it. We managed."

It wasn't all dishonest day's work for the boys. Steve endured a variety of menial jobs: dishwasher, bowling alley janitor, lawn mower and pizza maker. Izzy was briefly employed in a guitar shop, and Slash did time in a clock factory. Axl did telephone sales and held a position as night manager at a Tower Video outlet. To help make ends meet, Axl and Slash volunteered as medical test subjects for UCLA, smoking cigarettes for $8 an hour.

Meanwhile, Guns N' Roses staked quite a reputation for themselves locally. Slash asserts, "When we first were a club band in Hollywood, we were sort of a sore thumb on the glam scene – in the middle of it, but at the same time, not into it at all. We put across kind of a 'f*ck you' attitude, and that gave the band a foundation."

"You fight for your place," states Axl. "I remember two years of standing at the Troubadour and talking to no one, everybody thinking they're so cool. Eventually we did our own thing, made new friends and brought a new crowd to the Troubadour."

"We just kept playing," says Izzy "and we made so much noise in the city . . . that the labels started to come to us. *They* came to *us*! They would come over to the studio and come in the alley and see drunks . . . and the next thing you know we're going to their office! We made them take us all out for dinner for like a week or two and we started eating good! We'd order all this food and drink and say, Okay, talk!"

As outside interest burgeoned, so did the lawsuits – ranging from the former "manager" who wanted a chunk of major label pie, to supposed trumped-up rape charges, allegedly stemming from a disgruntled ex-girlfriend. "Everyone was trying to hide it from the record company," says Axl. " 'Rape charge? What rape charge?' The charges were dropped eventually, but for a while we had to go into hiding. We had undercover cops and the vice squad looking for us. They were talking a mandatory five years. It kind of settled my hormones for a while."

Early in their career, Vicky Hamilton housed band members (and their equipment) in her cramped West Hollywood apartment, booked shows for them, and generally lent support to the band. Slash once stated in an interview that prior to Vicky's involvement, there was no label interest. "She was the only person that way back when we were doin' our first gigs – she'd say, 'You guys are *great*; you're gonna make it.' I've gotta tip my hat to her."

Later in their career, Axl sang a different tune about their unofficial ex-manager, explaining that Vicky Hamilton, "basically had a monopoly on booking bands at the Roxy and the Whiskey, and we needed to get those gigs. We also needed a place to live. Vicky offered us help. She said she'd get us $25,000 we desperately needed for the proper equipment to start getting close to the sound we wanted."

Guns N' Roses claim Vicky never forked out the cash; Vicky insisted on a cut of their future earnings, based on her purported $10,000 investment. A year later, she sued the band for a million bucks.

Amidst legal threats and a rumour maelstrom, Guns N' Roses released their first record in December of '86, a self-produced EP on their own Uzi-Suicide label, entitled *Live?!* @ Like A Suicide*. Without any advertising, it sold over 10,000 copies in four weeks and became an instant collector's item.

KISS's Paul Stanley expressed interest in the band; at one point he discussed production with Axl and Slash and listened to the demo they'd done with Spencer Proffer; but according to Axl, "He wanted to rewrite two of our very favourite songs, so it was over right then and there."

Slash remembers a night when Paul Stanley attended one of their shows and ". . . hung out where we hang out. I'm looking at this guy watching what we do. He's a nice guy, but he didn't have a clue as to what we were doing. Everyone gets the basic idea: They're a rock 'n' roll Band. But they don't get the formula."

Guns N' Roses finally inked the dotted line on March 26, 1986 with Geffen Records, label of David Geffen, an old family friend of Slash and his parents. Izzy maintains that the reason Guns N' Roses opted for Geffen was because "They were the coolest; they were very hip to what was going on. They know about rock n' roll. There were labels we went to who didn't know who f*ckin' Aerosmith was, that wanted to sign us. At one label, something came up about Steven Tyler, and this chick said, 'Who's that?' " Geffen A&R man Tom Zutaut, impressed by the Guns' ability to play louder than AC/DC, was the first major label executive they felt they could talk turkey with. Axl admits, "He's the main reason our record happened."

Appetite For Destruction, the resulting debut LP, got its title from a postcard the Guns spotted in a shop. The cover artwork, depicting what appeared to be a robot rapist and its dishevelled female victim, was condemned by several major record chains who refused to stock the LP, thereby prompting Geffen Records to remove it. "We liked the artwork," affirms Axl, "But it wasn't something that we felt so strongly about that we'd die for it. After the first few thousand copies, it was changed to our logo."

Produced and engineered by Mike Clink (veteran of Triumph and UFO sessions), and mixed by Steve Thompson and Michael Barbiero, *Appetite for Destruction* was released in July '87, but took ten months just to crack Billboard's Top 100. The disc needed something to help push it into people's faces; ironically, a man representing law n' order provided the impetus for Guns N' Roses next move.

The Dead Pool, starring Clint Eastwood as Dirty Harry, featured Guns N' Roses' acting debut – all ten seconds of it. Hardly a "big break" into the movies, the Guns' onscreen activities proved largely incidental.

Slash summarizes their "role" in the plot of the film: "Y'see the movie's about this kind of betting thing where people bet on who is going to die, only they start fixing the bets. So, there's this rock star guy who's a junkie; his name's Johnny Squares, hahaha . . . So, he's a junkie and someone laces his dope. He dies of what looks like an overdose. So of course, Clint, being Dirty Harry and all, gets hip to what's going on. We're like friends of this dead rock star. (They picked the perfect band, I guess.) So anyway, we're in the funeral procession and we're shaking all these relatives' hands and sh*t.

"The next scene we did was a pain in the ass. This Johnny Squares guy, besides being a rock star, is also this kind of D-grade horror movie star. He dies during the making of one of these films and the director just continues shooting and making the movie. So the part we're in is sort of like extra extras. Actually, this scene is real cool. Me and Duff and Izzy are up on this boat. It's like a horror movie, right? So it's this fuckin' death boat. It had real skeletons on it . . . Imagine – it's bad enough you die and then your skeleton ends up in a movie."

According to Slash, the Guns' introduction to Mr. Eastwood didn't exactly make their day: "He comes up to us like someone forced him to do it and says, 'Hey, great album' and then he just walks away." Slash does concede, however, that Clint is "a pretty menacing character".

While Guns N' Roses cameo in *The Dead Pool* amounted to a big "so what?", the movie's theme song, composed and performed by the band, raised more than a few eyebrows. "Welcome To The Jungle" and its accompanying video, blasted raw, fresh air into 1988's stale metal/rock doldrums. A thrilling introduction to the band, "Welcome" was many kids' first glimmering of Guns N' Roses unmitigated musical power and onstage ferocity; and like all their songs, it was rooted in harsh autobiographical truth. "I slept one night in a schoolyard in Queens with a big fence around it," recounts Axl. "This black guy came up to me and said, 'You know where you are? You in the jungle! You gonna die!' So we put that in [the] song."

"Welcome To the Jungle" was Axl and Slash's first co-written effort. "I wrote the words in Seattle," Axl remembers. 'It's a big city, but at the same time, it's still a small city compared to L.A. and the things you're gonna learn . . . I just wrote how L.A. looked to me. If someone comes to town and they want to find something, they can find whatever they want."

The video for "Welcome", shot mostly in a downtown L.A. hotel, quickly became an MTV fave, and FM radio stations meekly slipped the song some airplay; but it was the group's scintillating live shows that established them as a force to be reckoned with. No mere opening act, the Guns scorched the earth wheresoever they traipsed, winning more converts than Billy Graham on Judgement Day. The word was out: Guns N' Roses were "the next big thing".

Following brief outings with the Cult and EZO, GN'R scored a major coup by hooking up with a Mötley Crüe tour. Musically and ethically, the Crüe met with Slash's approval: "[Mötley] are cool, I have a lot of respect for them. They're really sincere." Members of Guns N' Roses got on famously with the Crüe, comparing tales of wanton behaviour and generally trying to out-do each other's exploits and excesses. "Nikki and I go back a long way," Slash remembers, referring to his various encounters with Sixx while hanging outside clubs where the Mötley guy's band performed.

Heartwarming though it may have been for Guns N' Roses to tour with the rock acts they were raised on, the band's unruly road behaviour prompted second thoughts for many a headliner and promoter alike: There was the Doubletree Hotel incident in Dallas, Texas. "I got really drunk and *destroyed* a room," explains Slash. "They had cops after us. Our road manager had to do some fast talking to get us out of that one."

On returning from the Mötley tour, Guns N' Roses played a chaotic show at L.A.'s Cathouse. The festivities nearly came to a premature halt when Axl was arrested halfway through the second song of the set for leaping into the crowd and fighting with a security guard who was hassling a friend of theirs for no apparent reason. Though Axl had been hauled off to the slammer, the band saw there was no getting offstage amidst the brouhaha, so they decided to ad-lib the remainder of the show. A roadie was persuaded to shriek "Communication Breakdown" and Izzy graced the crowd with his vocal rendition of a few Rolling Stones classics. Slash topped off the evening's entertainment with a 15 minute guitar solo.

When Guns N' Roses missed a Phoenix date scheduled for the end of a small concert hall headlining tour due to an unspecified illness that had Axl hospitalized, the rumour-mongers had a field day. Amidst stories ranging from Axl's death by O.D., to the demise of the entire band, Guns N' Roses were abruptly informed that they were cancelled from the upcoming David Lee Roth tour they'd planned on joining. A proposed AC/DC tour also fell through. While cancellations are nothing unusual for the music business, the controversy Guns N' Roses generated at this early stage of their concert career was a bit out of line.

"The press really jumped on the tour stories," said Slash, "but the fact is that each time we lost a tour, we ended up with a better one. I mean, we were able to tour with bands like Mötley Crüe and Aerosmith, which was a dream come true for us. They gave us a chance, and we'll always remember that."

Although they landed a slot on Alice Cooper's tour, their troubles were far from over. Slash recalls: "After the Mötley Crüe tour was over, we went out with Alice Cooper 'cause we didn't want to go home. What else happened? Steve broke his hand. There were shows getting cancelled like here and there and then we had three days off in

Muskegon, Michigan. There's *nada*, there's nothing there. It's like living in a mall. So the last day, we were supposed to have left around three in the afternoon. At about nine p.m., me, Steve, Duff and Tyler the security guard were sitting in this bar, and Steve's had like 15 Kamikazes by then. Anyway, he flew off the handle at something and got thrown out of the bar. He tried to punch a lamp post, the glass part, and he punched the metal part and broke his hand." While his hand healed, Cinderella drummer Fred Coury completed Steve's tour obligations.

On the subsequent Iron Maiden tour, Guns N' Roses managed to enhance their reputation for unreliability even further. Mid-tour, Duff was replaced by ex-Cult bassist Haggis. The reason? The durned fool was gettin' hitched!

Duff first met his future bride Mandy Brix, Japanese restaurant hostess and lead singer for L.A.'s The Lame Flames, on her birthday. Gallant, though unprepared, Duff didn't have a gift, so he immediately whipped off his sunglasses and bestowed them upon her. "I knew then it was serious," Mandy said. On May 28, 1988, over the Memorial Day weekend the happy couple were joined in matrimonial bliss. As the wedding date had been set before the Maiden tour was confirmed, Duff was unable to cancel and his bandmates were forced to skip the ceremony.

All through the tour, Axl was plagued with vocal problems due to polyps in his throat. With another road stint looming on the horizon, Axl was sent off to recover, "because we didn't want to fuck up the Aerosmith tour," says Slash.

Even Guns N' Roses "dream tour" with Aerosmith had its moments of tribulation. Doug Goldstein, the Guns' tour manager for that jaunt remembers, "In Philadelphia, Axl was coming to the show a little late. When Axl and his brother come to pull in, Stuart, Axl's brother, jumps out of the car and pulls the parking cones out of the way so they can get in. He tells the parking guy he's got the lead singer in the car. The guy tells Stuart to fuck off. Axl doesn't want that to happen – he's one of the most loyal people I've encountered – so he jumps out and gets into it with the parking attendant. It turned into a pretty big scene. So the lead singer's being taken to jail with a half hour to go before the show . . . I practically had to blow every cop within a five-mile radius to get him out of jail." Axl made the gig with five minutes to spare.

By far the most unfortunate mishap to befall Guns N' Roses was the incident at the 1988 Castle Donington 'Monsters of Rock' Festival, at which two teenagers, 18-year-old Alan Dick and 20-year-old Landon Siggers, were trampled to death during Guns' performance before a crowd of 107,000. Just prior to the gig, Duff had expressed the sentiment that, "You're making history if you play Donington." However, the only history made at this performance was of the most tragic sort. As soon as the band mounted the stage, fans surged forward and crushed audience members in the stampede to the front.

Slash delivered an eyewitness account immediately after the show: "It was real scarey . . . It was kids piled on kids horizontal on the ground. They were unconscious. And more people kept falling on them. I saw them. It took about 20 minutes to get everybody out. We stopped the show and they finally pulled the last couple of people out and I think they were dead. It was really weird. I saw no life in those bodies at all."

Although such incidents can happen anywhere, Slash opined that English audiences have more of an edge to them: "American crowds are really cool. British crowds tend to be more hectic, more insane. That's the big difference. I think the Brits are more starved for it. They have to go through more hell with life in general. In America, everybody just gets into it because they want to have a good time. In England, they're desperate for it because the rest of life is pretty screwed up. I was born here and I know middle class in Britain is not happening, y'know?"

Duff summed up the band's frustration and anger over the accident: "When kids die at a gig, that's a little . . . the screwed up thing about it is it's a sort of a Catch-22, because you want to have that element of danger and stuff, and you want to have that sort of chaotic you-don't-know-what's-going-to-happen-next kind of thing happening, but then when people really do get hurt, or somebody dies from it, then you feel sort of responsible, and you just hate to, because a rock n' roll show is really supposed to be about having a good time. It was originally supposed to bring people together. So, it just sort of blows the whole thing. It's great to go out there and really kick ass, but then that kind of energy that you're putting into it also sort of generates another kind of energy that is not necessarily happening. And, you can't control it."

In its 50th week on the American charts, *Appetite For Destruction* hit the number one spot; almost a year later, it jumped up to number one again. Not since Led Zeppelin's first album has a debut LP by a rock band sold as phenomenally without first releasing a single; by the spring of '89, *Appetite's* sales surpassed quintuple platinum. What do the boys have to say about this phenomenal response to their first album? "I thought we made a good Motorhead record," humbly opines Slash.

When the first single from the album, 'Sweet Child O' Mine", also achieved number one status, Slash modestly deemed its success a "fluke", insisting that Guns N' Roses only released it at the behest of their record company. Further, GN'R weren't too pleased with the notion of doing an edit for the radio. Slash tried to see the positive side of this compromise: "If it will make that many more people aware of us who normally wouldn't be, then cool."

While working on "Sweet Child O' Mine", Axl took a little journey back to his musical roots: "I'm from Indiana where Lynyrd Skynyrd were considered God to the point that you ended up saying, 'I hate this fucking band!' Yet it was to tapes of those hoary rebel minstrels that Axl bravely returned, checking "to make sure we'd got that down home heartfelt feeling."

"The thing about 'Sweet Child,' " laughs Duff, "it was written in five minutes. It was one of those songs, only three chords. You know that guitar lick Slash does at the beginning? It was kinda like a joke because we thought, 'What is this song? It's gonna be nothin', it'll be filler on the record.' And except that vocal-wise, it's very sweet and sincere, Slash was fuckin' around when he first wrote that lick."

A love song composed for his current girlfriend, model Erin Everly, (daughter of Don, of Everly Brothers fame) Axl recalls the spontaneous origins of the tune: "I had written this poem, reached a dead end with it and put it on the shelf. Then Slash and Izzy got working together on songs and I came in, Izzy hit a rhythm, and all of a sudden this poem popped into my head. It just all came together. A lot of rock bands are too fucking wimpy to have any sentiment or any emotion in any of their stuff unless they're in pain. It's the first positive love song I've ever written, but I never had anyone to write anything that positive about, I guess."

Axl's relationship with Erin, which he compares to that of The Doors' Jim Morrison and his girlfriend Pamela Courson, is tender, deep and volatile. "They were always fighting, but they were soulmates. That's how I feel about Erin." Erin, for her part, found Axl strange when they first met, but admits, "I was attracted to him." Their erratic relationship has endured intermittently for several years now, because Axl says, "We have so many things in common, it's weird. No matter what happens, we're somehow always gonna be together."

The seeds of GN'R's follow-up single, 'Paradise City', pre-date the band's existence; Duff first came up with the chord changes on moving to L.A., ". . . When I didn't know anybody and was kinda feeling down . . . Like reaching for something, you know?" A collaborative effort, 'Paradise City" was germinated by Duff, but nurtured to full fruition by the entire band. "If one person brings in a song to this band," Duff notes, "it always gets raped by the other four people. It always gets changed around to where it's Guns N' Roses."

"The verses are more about being in the jungle," explains Axl. "The chorus is like being back in the Midwest or somewhere. It reminds me of when I was a little kid and just looked up at the blue sky and went, 'Wow, what is all this? It's so big out there.' Everything was more innocent. There are parts of the song that have more of a down home feel and when I started putting down the over-layers of my vocals (I put five tracks on there), it seemed that it came out like some Irish or Scottish heritage.

"One of the weird things is I had a feeling that it would go over good in Europe. The kids there sang 'Brownstone', they sang 'It's So Easy', 'Mama Kin' and these other songs that they'd heard on the EP. They also sang 'Paradise City' and they'd never heard it." Adds Izzy, "They sang as loud as our stage monitors. We could hear them over the monitors."

GN'R Lies (subtitled *The Sex, The Drugs, The Violence, The Shocking Truth*) was released by Geffen Records on November 30, 1988. Containing on one side a re-issue of the Uzi-Suicide EP *Live?!* @ Like A Suicide* (of which only 25,000 were originally pressed) and four newly recorded acoustic numbers on the flip, *GN'R Lies* served as an interim respite for Guns fans hungrily awaiting another LP.

"We wanted to put something out between the last tour and the next album," explains Slash. "We also heard that kids were having to pay $50 to $100 for the original *Live?!* @ Like A Suicide*. And we wanted to do some new songs that show another side of us. These are songs we just felt like doing. Yes, this is a rock n' roll band, but there are a lot of different influences within Guns N' Roses. We write a lot of our songs on acoustic guitar. So doing *Lies* seemed a natural thing for us."

The album artwork, designed to resemble a tabloid magazine cover, is the Guns' ironic response to the incessant rumours surrounding them. "We've been the centre of attention and hype and sensationalism," Slash states, "And all of it is bullshit. We've heard that we've all died in a car crash, that we've done this or that. This was our chance to turn it around and stick it back in their faces."
Guns N' Roses have proven time and again that they can transcend any hype, any rumour, any setback that destiny dishes out. Onstage they're truly in their element; emerging to face the throng: fans and foes alike are blown away by the sheer sonic onslaught of their performance.

An early Guns concert at New York's Ritz left a powerful impression on their initially sceptical audience, including producer Daniel Rey (Iggy Pop, The Ramones, and Circus of Power) who remembers, "When they came out, everyone just looked at each other. They knew they were seeing the next big band, the next big thing for the '90s . . . They had the aura of what everybody tries to be. They had a natural sort of confidence that nobody has had since [early] Van Halen, the kind of thing you can't imitate. People like Bon Jovi are more, like, manufactured. They portray something without [really] being it. Guns N' Roses are the only ones who just *are*."

Top charting international mega-stars Guns N' Roses' careers have progressed profoundly from opening the Troubadour's weekday slots; but they've steadfastly maintained the same attitude all along. "We're honest," avers Slash, "not a façade of rock n' roll to look good in magazines."

"Put yourself in our position," suggests Duff, "You can't really explain it. We're still the same guys. People expect us to be different. But the only thing that's different is we sold six or seven million records!"

"We've never written a song for anyone but ourselves," not to sound selfish, but we just haven't. We're a rock and roll band. We're not a band that goes, 'Okay, let's write a commercial song.' We despise that. But it just happened." Issues of integrity and commercialism not withstanding, for Guns N' Roses it's happened, in aces, spades, platinum and diamonds.

"I'm sorry, I'm not catering to the masses," W. Axl Rose sums up. "We're in this band for ourselves, and if everybody else likes it, that's cool too, and that adds to it. But we're playing what *we* want to hear. The main trick will be to come off not sounding like pompous assholes."

When 'G N'R Lies' joined 'Appetite For Destruction' in the US Top Five in February 1989, it made them the first band in the eighties to have two albums in the top five at the same time. Many people were surprised by the acoustic nature of the newer songs on 'Lies', but that's exactly how much of the material started life – on tour in Slash's hotel room, to be precise. "I sit in bed with the TV turned down staring at the ceiling," he revealed, "coming up with stuff in my head trying to make things work. I put a lot of ideas on tape. It never stops . . ."

An eye-opening version of the live crowd-pleaser 'You're Crazy', originally heard on 'Appetite' gave more hints as to the G N'R hitmaking technique. Written just after the band had signed their recording contract, it was now slowed down to its original tempo "for the sake of something to do," claimed Slash. But it was a long, long way from there to the red-hot riffing of the savage 'One In A Million', a song that was to cause trouble further down the line.

Never afraid to display their influences, the band were happy to stand by their own distinctive versions of 'Mama Kin' (from the Aerosmith songbook) and Oz-rockers Rose Tattoo's 'Nice Boys (Don't Play Rock'n'Roll)' which, along with 'Reckless Life' and 'Move To The City' comprised the previously-released 'Suicide' side. A brace of new cuts in 'Patience', soon to be a hit single, and 'Used To Love Her' (described as "a joke" – *some* joke!) balanced the mini-album at four tracks a side.

The fans had another hot platter to savour . . . yet the hits from the first album just kept on a-comin'. 'Paradise City' hit number five in the US charts in March, reaching number six in Britain during April. The following month 'Sweet Child O' Mine' was re-released in Britain, this time reaching number six, while in June it was the turn of 'Patience' from 'Lies' which made number four in the US, and number ten in the UK.

Guns N'Roses were enjoying the 'Bon Jovi' factor as the rock band to catch the imagination of the mass pop audience. But the backlash was not long in making itself felt. In August, G N'R hit the headlines for the wrong reasons when they were sensationally dropped from an AIDS benefit bill in New York, due to the controversial lyrics of 'One In A Million', one of the new cuts on 'Lies'. References to 'faggots' got the benefit organisers hot under the collar, but a parallel mention of 'niggers' understandably upset Slash, a child of mixed-race parents. "I said I didn't think it was really cool," he admits, "but Axl gets very adamant . . . I don't regret doing 'One In A Million' . . . but now everybody's homing in on that one line, and I can't complain because I understand why . . . there's nothing I can say that's going to change it."

THE
AMERICAN MUSIC
AWARDS

But worse was to come . . . Two months on, Axl shocked the Los Angeles Coliseum crowd - not to mention G N'R fans the world over – by announcing his retirement on stage as the band opened a series of showcase gigs with The Rolling Stones, accusing certain members of the band of "Dancing with 'Mr Brownstone'." The echoes of that announcement were heard around the rock world . . . and not least close to home.

The following night, Slash came to the microphone for a rare statement, publicly promising to clean up and sort his own personal problems out. "The one thing I care about mostly in my life – the band – was blowing apart," he confessed later. "That was the major incentive." Along with drugs, he also vowed to cut down on the drink habit that encompassed "one or two bottles of Jack Daniels a night . . . sometimes half a gallon."

And not before time, either . . . When Slash and Duff were invited to the 1990 American Music Awards, no-one tipped them off that they'd carry off two trophies. Slash was delegated to pick them up – and in doing so dropped a number of f-words on national live TV. "Out of all the people there, we were the only ones not putting on a façade," he insisted.

With the media declaring open season on G N'R, and Slash in particular, perhaps one of the people with a real insight was his mother Ola Hudson. "A lot of things I've read make it seem like he never had a family and grew up in the streets like an urchin. But that's not true. It's just part of the image. He's not all leather and tattoos."

If Slash had his problems, 1989 wasn't a red-letter year for Izzy either. He got himself into a fight in a Los Angeles TV studio with Motley Crue singer Vince Neil after Neil's wife accused him of making advances. He was temporarily banged to rights – and, to add injury to insult, his cellmate gave him a black eye!

Another brush with the law followed an in-flight fracas when, after waiting 15 minutes for the men's room on a US airliner, Izzy decided he could wait no longer. He was jailed for two days on landing and fined $3,200 for 'interfering with the duties' of the plane's crew! His reaction to trouble was to go on the run. As he explained during a flying European visit: "You could say I've been living in exile for the last seven or eight months. I'll travel here, go on there – I haven't got a regular place where I stay!"

Fame and fortune had turned on the band, making every visit to a club the opportunity for someone to make their name by decking a Gunner. Axl got into a backstage fight with British glam-rockers Dogs D'Amour at Los Angeles' Club With No Name, emerging with a bloody nose. Duff, meanwhile, was attacked without warning by a nightclub bouncer in New Orleans – but returned with his 11-man entourage and had the *bouncer* bounced out!

Meanwhile, Axl's life was rapidly becoming a living nightmare. He was arrested on suspicion of assault when his neighbour accused him of breaking a bottle on her head. He'd already complained of mistreatment by two policemen investigating loud music at his apartment some months earlier. The bottle case was thrown out of court, but Axl and Erin Everly parted. The stormy relationship saw their new home come in for The Who's famous hotel-room treatment, press reports suggested, with thousands of dollars' worth of damage being done. "What was really wild," commented Axl, "was when Erin went back next day to finish the job."

Axl's moods were clearly the cause of some friction within the band. And while his commitment to the cause was rarely questioned, Axl's brief 'notice to quit' served during those epic gigs with the Stones was evidence to prove he was quite prepared to go solo if and when circumstances dictated. Interestingly, he'd said as much in a 1988 interview with a small-circulation musicians' magazine. "I don't want to go solo but there are areas I'd like to explore – maybe movies – where I might not be able to stay in the band to do it."

His troubled marriage to Erin Everly couldn't be put down 100 per cent to media attention, but it's not easy to solve problems in the glare of the public gaze. And the pressures of fame were clearly getting to him: his $1.8 million Hollywood home was guarded by no fewer than 20 security guards, he screened all callers by a video camera and apparently kept a pistol and semi-automatic rifle by his bedside.

THE ATTITUDE

JACK DANIEL'S
WHISKEY

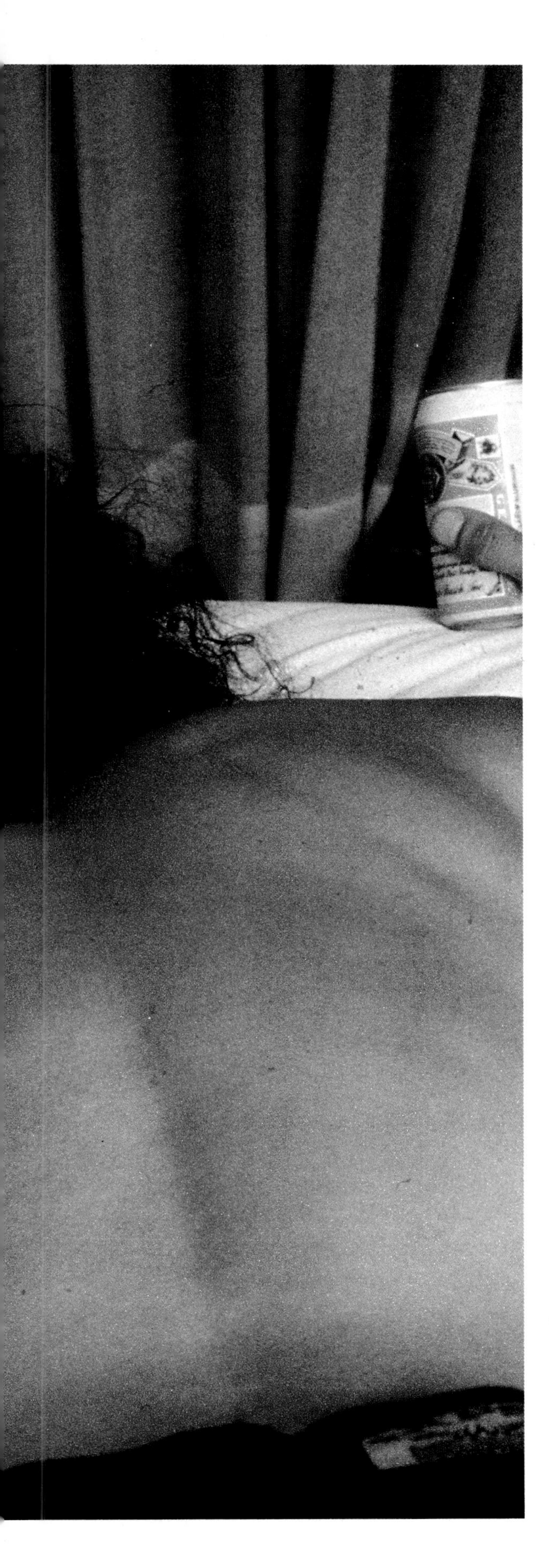

No-one was sorry to see the back of 1989 – an eventful year for many reasons, most of them unrelated to music. 1990 started promisingly in April with an appearance at the Farm Aid III charity show in Indianapolis, where the showstopper was an unlikely but highly appropriate cover version – 'Down On The Farm' by British punk veterans the UK Subs.

But the horseshit was to hit the fan in a big way in July when drummer Steven Adler finally made his exit. When the move came it wasn't a total surprise. After all, two temporary replacements, Cinderella's Fred Coury and Sea Hags' Adam Maples, had previously filled in on tour – though he *had* been back in the ranks at Farm Aid III on April 7.

Rehearsals for the long-awaited new record were finally taking place – but when Axl and Duff complained that Steven's erratic timekeeping was holding up the proceedings, a newly cleaned-up Slash finally admitted he couldn't defend his childhood friend any more. "We waited for him for a year . . . how long is a band supposed to wait around? All he lived for was sex, drugs and rock'n'roll. Then it was drugs and rock'n'roll. Then it was just drugs."

First contender for the hottest seat in rock was the already tried Adam Maples, " . . . a real cool guy," according to Slash, "but he just didn't have the right *vibe*." The Pretenders had been one of the groups to make a real impression on the early G N'R line-up – and when drummer Martin Chambers applied for the gig, it seemed like a marriage made in heaven . . . But despite the vibe being better this time, it didn't work out. "Martin played with them a couple of times," a band spokesman said, "and at first they thought he would be a good stand-in if Steven wasn't ready for live work, because he had more experience of playing to big audiences in stadiums." But that, clearly, was as far as it went.

As hope began to fade, Slash caught a gig at the local Universal Amphitheatre by The Cult, the British band that had toured with the Gunners on their first coast-to-coast tour. He straightaway homed in on drummer Matt Sorum – and liked what he saw, concluding that "it wouldn't hurt to try him . . . Thank God I went to that show that night," he continued. "The fact that Matt could play and fit in is what saved us. If we hadn't found somebody it would ultimately have been the demise of the band. Matt's been capable of keeping up with it, if not enhancing it totally, and bringing new stuff to it."

Another new recruit swelled the G N'R ranks to six when previously unknown keyboardist Dizzy Reed took a bow. Immediately confirmed as a permanent member and likely to appear on record sleeves, his arrival lent their music a greater width, freeing Izzy to duel axes with Slash as the keyboards held down the middle range.

Confirmation of this on record was to be a long time in coming, since Guns N'Roses' only two vinyl outings of the year had both already been recorded with the earlier, legendary five-piece line-up. An apocalyptic cover version of Dylan's 'Knockin' On Heaven's Door' was their distinctive contribution to the mega-hit *Days Of Thunder* soundtrack, while the altogether more uptempo 'Civil War' appeared that summer on 'Nobody's Child', a charity fund-raising album for Romanian orphans put together by George Harrison and his wife Olivia. It was fitting that the guitarist of the sixties' greatest band had approached the nineties' biggest names to help out in this worthy cause, proving once again that, despite the press image, their collective heart was most certainly in the right place.

Sorum and Reed made their Guns N'Roses stage débuts on 18 January 1991 – not at some low-key bar-band gig, but with typical panache at Brazil's International, satellite-televised Rock in Rio Festival alongside Judas Priest and a star-studded bill. With the eyes of the whole world upon them, they took the stage at the vast Maracana stadium, home of the Brazilian World Cup soccer legends – and scored straight away with a team performance of staggering intensity and swaggering bravado.

As the opening chords of 'All Tied Up' rang around the stadium, Axl strutted and posed with the appetite of a master showman starved of public acclaim for far too long, while Matt Sorum laid the foundations of an earth-shattering sound with a four-square rock rhythm. And in the electric guitar department Slash, Izzy and Duff were sparking as never before.

Despite the delays, this wasn't a clinically over-rehearsed performance, by any manner of means. Reed, for one, had yet to work himself into each and every song: with typical offhandedness, Axl suggested he played percussion on a track he'd never played on before! Clearly the musical philosophy best expressed by Duff remained, as ever, a down to earth one. "None of us are the greatest technical musicians, you know: we all have big technical holes. We'll never be like Rush, we'll never be that good. But I think we're way more honest. In some ways it's a calling of a rebel spirit to kids. 'Cause we ***always*** do what we want."

The long-awaited new LP 'Use Your Illusion' had been scheduled for April 1991 release, but was postponed for three months when mastermixer Bill Price (who'd worked with long-time G N'R influences The Sex Pistols and The Pretenders, among others) was called in to add the icing on the musical cake. The single, 'Don't Cry', runaway chart success proved that this was one group who had certainly not forgotten.

In the end, 'Use Your Illusion' appeared as two double slabs of vinyl, each in a wide-spine single sleeve. Cassette and compact disc-owning fans got a single item. And there was certainly no shortage of material for what was without doubt the most eagerly awaited new record since Def Leppard's 'Hysteria' four years earlier. With Mike Clink again in the producer's chair, the songs they recorded reflected the problems of the past: Slash describes the mood of the LP as "pretty pissed off...there's not a ton of really happy material on it."

Fully three dozen songs had been committed to tape in 30 frantic days, each and every one to be used on album, EP or as a B-side/12-inch bonus. Horns, sitars, mandolins and other exotic influences were here, there and everywhere. As well as new material and a clutch of covers, the band had revived a few punky staples of their early stage set like 'Ain't Goin' Down' and 'Back Off, Bitch' that long-time fans claimed, no ***insisted***, were as good as anything that's come since.

The newer songs gave Slash and Co the chance to stretch out, especially 'November Rain' and the anti-drug 'Coma' - both 10 minutes long "and with 300 chord changes", according to Slash. 'Rain' was distinguished by Slash's long, languid guitar outro that takes off in 'Layla' vein, while the lyrics of 'Coma' had an all-too-familiar inspiration.

'Pretty Tied Up', 'Double Takin' Jive' and the funky 'Bad Apples' had already been road-tested and rated among the standouts at the Rio show. Other likely candidates for final track selection included 'Dust and Bones', a raunchy slice of G N'R rock featuring Izzy's best Keith Richards impression; 'Shotgun Blues', a short, aggressive shot with punk overtones, and 'The Garden', a deadly duet featuring Axl and Alice Cooper. Further titles included 'Estranged', 'Locomotive', 'Don't Damn Me', '14 Years', 'You Ain't The First', 'So Fine' and, of course, the second single 'Don't Cry'.

A monster album could only mean one thing - a mammoth tour! Nothing less than a two-year world-girdling epic, indeed, planned to start in Australia and work its way around the known rock'n'roll world via New Zealand, Japan, Europe and the US. Slash, particularly, stated that he'd like to play "all those places we haven't done yet". What was more, with so many tracks already in the can, a 'new' G N'R album could be released halfway through the tour, with a live platter, scheduled for release as the tour finally ended.

Two years on the road didn't seem like a rest cure, exactly, but it was work – and given the problems that cropped up during the band's enforced leisure time, that was clearly something to savour.

The provocatively titled Get In The Ring Tour had, of course, been intended to coincide with the albums' release, but ended up previewing songs you couldn't yet buy. That wasn't the only disturbing factor: manager Alan Niven was fired when Axl apparently refused to finish the albums until co-manager Doug Goldstein replaced him. Then Izzy was leaving his German shepherd dog (complete with tour pass) to stand in for him backstage, leaving Axl to dub him 'Mr Invisible'. The guitarist also preferred to travel by himself rather than fly with the band, proclaiming "If you're driving or something, it keeps you in touch with the rest of the world."

That feeling was heightened by the fact that he was now leading a self-proclaimed drug and alcohol-free existence. "I don't miss it," he confided, adding ironically... "There's nothing like throwing up out of a bus door going 65 miles an hour." If Duff spoke for the others, Izzy was alone in his studied sobriety. "We're still not angels by any means. We still do... that sex, drugs and rock'n'roll thing. But it's not our lifestyle any more. We know how to choose what and where and when. We're not going to let it destroy the band... or us."

From the outset, the tour was dogged by bad crowd behaviour. In Indiana, Axl compared the audience to prisoners in Auschwitz Nazi concentration camp. Fans at Alpine Valley ripped up newly-laid turf and pelted the stage. Tempers ran high, too, when Axl was two hours late on stage at New York's Nassau Coliseum when, he claimed, the record company delayed him by insisting he do a prestigious, pre-gig ***Rolling Stone*** photo session. Shows at Tacoma and Dallas were stopped in full flow as Axl berated the bottle-throwers, and worse. "This is not about us being badder than you or anything," he insisted. "It has to do with being responsible - both to the band and to yourselves."

The worst incident of all occurred at the St Louis Riverport Arts Centre in July when Axl leapt from the stage to confiscate a camera from a biker. Duff was twice hit by bottles before the band retired - intending, Matt Sorum explained afterwards, to return to the stage when things had calmed down. Instead, the crowd took matters into their own hands and trashed the equipment in a frightening stage invasion: shows in Illinois and Kansas City had to be cancelled as replacement gear was procured. "One of Izzy's amps we found out by the concession stands," marvelled Slash.

According to manager Goldstein, "The primary problem was a motorcycle club that was intimidating people in the audience. One of them also happened to have a still camera. Axl kept asking local security to get rid of them. I found out after the show that these guys are all friends of local security..." He concluded that... "Axl has never been one to stand by and watch an injustice being done to his fans" - but this wouldn't stop the incident rebounding on band and singer nearly a year later. For the present, Axl had enough on his plate: a sharp-eyed critic at an LA concert spotted he had an autocue to help him master the pile of new lyrics he had to contend with.

'You Could Be Mine', the first single released as a taster for the forthcoming feast, was used in the Arnold Schwarzenegger film ***Terminator II***, something Slash, for one, later publicly regretted. Though reaching number 3 in Britain (with Arnie - but not Izzy - in the video), it failed to climb higher than 29 in the States, where G N'R's singles placings were inevitably a rung or three lower than in Britain. 'Don't Cry' would reach 8 in Britain, 10 in the States: a cover of Paul McCartney's 'Live And Let Die' 5 and 33, respectively, while the release of a fourth 45, 'November Rain', a British number 4, was put on hold at home.

European dates started in Helsinki on August 12, and saw the band take measures to stamp out the crowd violence that still seemed to follow them around. "Our own security director will be meeting each promoter," revealed Doug Goldstein, "and if we feel the promoter is not properly equipped we will bring in professional security people." This didn't stop a firecracker winging its way onstage in Copenhagen, where Axl declared a 15-minute music-free ceasefire before returning to insist... "We've found the guy. If you see anyone else throw anything at me, do me a favour - beat the fuck out of him."

Offstage, rumours of personnel problems - notably Matt and Izzy - dogged the tour. "The tensions get high at various points," explained Axl, "but Matt's working his ass off and he's great..." The rumour mill was silenced by the long-awaited arrival of 'Use Your Illusion' I & II in September 1991. "As far as the band is concerned," proclaimed Axl, "there have been no delays. The only rule we had was to make the best record we could, regardless of how long it took."

The delay and the headlines it - and the live shows - created had led to unprecedented demand. In the States, pre-orders broke four million (breaking Michael Jackson's two million record for 'Bad'), with another half-million sold on the day of release. The figures would have been even more impressive had two major chains, K Mart and Wal Mart, not blacked it, though Tower did their bit by opening at one minute past midnight on release day. The albums' arrival at numbers 1 and 2 in the British chart (in reverse order, as in the States) was the first time a single act had occupied the two top slots. Outselling Dire Straits by a ratio of two to one, they sold more in their first week of release than Metallica did in six.

Initial quantities of both albums carried a sticker stating: "This album contains language that some listeners may find objectionable. They can fuck off and buy something from the New Age section." And while there were inevitably dissenting voices here and there, 'Use Your Illusion I' and 'II' were devoured by the music business and press alike.

Melody Maker lauded 'I' as "a glossy rawness where every serrated edge etches itself into your brain... hard rock has never sounded so good," while 'II' was "nothing short of great art". Both carried versions of 'Don't Cry' (the lyrics differed), and though no other songs were duplicated there was a curious relationship between the first volume's 'Don't Damn Me' - in which Axl pleaded not to be judged - with 'II's 'Get In The Ring', in which hapless journalists who have had the temerity to criticise G N'R in the past were invited by name to put on the gloves. Throwbacks to The Rolling Stones (the feel of 'Coma') and Bob Dylan (another version of 'Knockin' On Heaven's Door') proved perhaps that despite all the rumoured punk covers - none of which were included - older influences still held good. ***New Musical Express*** found the albums too long-winded - "enough material between the two doubles to make one strong EP" - but the sheer variety on offer won over the majority of the critics.

Slash explained the 'double double album' concept: "Some of it's really old, so we just basically cleaned our whole slate. That way, when we do the next record we can start without any kind of a backlog." To charges of rip-off on a grand scale, Duff had this novel suggestion: "One kid can buy 'Volume I', one kid can buy 'Volume II' and they can tape off each others' records."

The rumour mill proved half right when the first leg of the Get In The Ring Tour ended with Izzy's departure. His decision to stay with ex-manager Alan Niven suggested he was less than happy with the (supposedly Axl-instigated) organisational changes that had been going on behind the scenes, let alone music matters. For his part, Axl believed... "Izzy never wanted something this big", but the guitarist's absence from the videos of 'Don't Cry' or 'You Could Be Mine' made his decision to quit something less than a surprise. His departure followed on the heels of a widely reported lawsuit from Steven Adler inferring that he'd been encouraged to do drugs to fit the band's image.

Meanwhile, Mötley Crüe's Vince Neil was taking the message of 'Get In The Ring' somewhat literally. "Last year on the MTV Awards pre-show, he challenged me to a fight, anytime, anyplace. Now's the time, Axl - unless you're all talk. Let's stop fighting in the press, put on the gloves in the ring and handle this man to man." Fellow rockers Eddie Van Halen and Sammy Hagar offered to stage the fight at Madison Square Garden following Neil's MTV outburst, but it didn't happen. Surprisingly for a man whose band was now demanding copy approval from every journalist it could persuade to sign a contract, Axl was busy confronting his personal devils elsewhere... in print.

In March 1992, ***Rolling Stone*** carried possibly the most revealing Axl Rose interview ever - and it made horrifying reading. He was undergoing therapy, he revealed, delving back into his past to reveal major problems. He claimed his mother had rejected him, picking "my stepfather over me ever since he was around and watched me get beaten by him." He blamed his grandmother's much-proclaimed anti-men feelings for his own misogynistic lyrics - "I've been hell on the women in my life and the women in my life have been hell on me".

Referring to his natural father (whom ***Rolling Stone*** believed dead), he claimed to have been drugged and sexually abused by him, this explaining accusations of being homophobic. His half-sister had been abused by his stepfather... the list of childhood horrors went on. These could all have been conveniently invented excuses for answering his critics, except that ***Rolling Stone*** had corroboration from his brother, sister and a family friend to back up Axl's claims.

When they hit the road again in early 1992, all eyes were on the new gun in Guns n'Roses - Gilby Clarke, who beat hot tips Dave Navarro (ex-Jane's Addiction) and Mick Cocks (ex-Rose Tattoo) to the most coveted spot in rock. MTV announced his recruitment mere hours after the little-known guitarist was asked to join the ranks - and though few outside LA had heard of his previous outfits, Pop Rockers Candy and - most recently - Rockers Kill For Thrill, he had links with the Gunners that stretched way back.

"Basically, I had known the band since they started," he explained. "I guess when it came up they kind of thought of me. Slash just called up and said 'Can you come down tomorrow and play?' and then he just said 'Can you come back tomorrow?' and 'Can you make it the next day?'... I didn't really realise that meant I was ***in the band***!"

Clarke's first week with the band was particularly traumatic. "I just didn't know what was going on because they were still calling up other guitar players... then I had another week to learn 40 songs and we were on tour!"

It was a close call... three weeks after starting auditions, the band were once more touring America coast-to-coast, for the first time without their lynchpin Izzy. In the style of the last days of Elvis, Axl's between-song rants were getting increasingly long and (self) abusive. The theme of 'Get In The Ring' had, it seemed, plainly not been exhausted. "Does anyone know how they write articles at ***Spin*** (magazine)? They pull themselves off (makes motion) and see what comes out!"

Musically, things were taking time to settle. ***Kerrang!*** reported of a Chicago concert that Slash was "playing more and more fast frills that add nothing," trading licks with Izzy's replacement "to the point of nauseous self-indulgence". Clarke, moreover, looked "more like a reject from the Black Crowes than an original sleaze-ball rocker".

As for the original sleaze-ball rockers, they were having a few problems of their own. Gigs in Chicago and Detroit were cancelled when the Chicago authorities indicated they would allow St Louis police to 'extradite' Axl and bust him outside state lines for the incident where they'd walked off stage at that city's Riverport Arts Centre after the row about security back in July 1991. Axl was, it seems, being held personally responsible for the thousands of dollars' damage to equipment and the venue itself. When the promoter warned the GN'R entourage, Chicago was cancelled at half an hour's notice, along with the following night's Detroit date. No news of rioting fans ***this*** time, thankfully...

The Freddie Mercury Tribute Show at London's Wembley Stadium in April provided a scheduled time-out from Stateside touring. It saw Slash share the bill for the first time ever with David Bowie, who'd once dated his mother. He told an interviewer how much he liked Bowie's Tin Machine ("They're great... they haven't done anything that blatantly sucks") and that he was busy writing the band's next album. How he and they would cope without the dependable Izzy's input remained to be seen: the departed ex-Gunner was, it was rumoured, already recording material in the vein of 'Use Your Illusion I's 'Dust And Bones' and about to sign with Geffen Records or its new DGC subsidiary.

Wembley was something of a triumph. They only managed two songs of a planned three-song set - 'Paradise City' and 'Knockin' On Heaven's Door', 'Sweet Child O'Mine' having been sacrificed for scheduling reasons - and the gaps for Axl to sermonise just weren't there. Yet from when he pranced on in his Union Jack jacket and white shorts, a real bolt of electricity shot through proceedings.

The line-up was considerably different to the one that'd torn up Wembley only the previous year: Dizzy Reed at the keyboards was augmented by a second player ("because sometimes on the record there are two piano parts"), a harmonica player ("Unfortunately none of us can play harmonica") and a couple of foxy female backing singers. The horn section they had been carrying with them, usually prominent on 'Live And Let Die', was absent. Their powerful performance of 'Heaven's Door', a tragically appropriate choice of song, was later issued as a British single (paired with the existing studio version), with proceeds going to the anti-Aids Terrence Higgins Trust; it peaked at number 2.

The band trooped off, having given their all - but that wasn't the end, as after various short sets were completed the stage was cleared for the main all-star gala event. Slash was first up, trading licks with Brian May as Def Leppard's Joe Elliott blustered his way through 'Tie Your Mother Down'. The two axemen hugged at the end of the song, an action that spoke volumes about the emotion level on stage.

Several numbers later, the crowd was hushed as the unmistakeable piano chords of 'Bohemian Rhapsody' rang out, the spotlight on a newly thatched Elton John. The stage was plunged into semi-darkness for the middle, taped section - and when the lights came up, Axl was already en route to centre stage. Less revealingly dressed than previously but now resplendent in a black leather kilt and matching mesh top with a number 22 in white, he linked arms with Elton for the final slow section - the most unlikely double act rock had, perhaps, ever seen. Militant gay groups had registered their disgust at Axl taking part at all, given the 'One In A Million' controversy, but Elton for one seemed to be prepared to forgive and forget.

Rose stayed there for an impassioned 'We Will Rock You', while all 98 musicians involved joined Liza Minnelli in a final chorus of 'We Are The Champions', bringing down the curtain on a memorable day - and one in which Guns N'Roses had played their part.

It had been an emotional occasion all round. Slash came off stage to be confronted by sexagenarian sex-goddess Elizabeth Taylor. "I ripped off my T-shirt, full of sweat," he explained later, "turned around and there she was in all her spangles. But we shook hands. She was cool." For Gilby Clarke... "It was a great time. We really appreciated them having us 'cos we're all Queen fans; it was pretty special."

The addition of the new man - happily married to the stunning Daniella - was, if anything, likely to be a stabilising factor. Clarke himself explained the logic behind the selection. Izzy, he said, "wasn't into it, and he hadn't been for a while. I don't think I would've been the guitar player to have started with them, but I might be the guitar player to take them where they might be going." Another plus point in his favour was that he'd been principal songwriter in his former band. "Obviously, I'd be into it," was his comment on the prospect of writing for his new outfit.

UK
YOUR

On his return from England, Slash had got up to jam with Los Angeles favourites Soundgarden, adding a long guitar solo to 'Slaves & Bulldozers'. Mind you, if press reports were to be believed it was a miracle he was there at all. He'd signed a £300,000 contract to endorse the delightfully named Black Death vodka - the proceeds of that deal helping pay for his new $1 million Hollywood home, rather than liquid refreshment - while he'd also been bitten by one of his snakes. "Rumour is the snake is feeling rather worse than Slash," one paper commented sourly. Elsewhere, he'd filled in tourless days playing sessions for Bob Dylan, Michael Jackson, Lenny Kravitz... the list went on.

Slash seemed to be edging Axl from the spotlight - but not *quite*... He'd apparently spent a cool £32,000 on a Mercedes for on-off girlfriend, model Stephanie Seymour - who was at the centre of one of Axl's typical manufactured mysteries when in a video dream sequence he 'married' her. Was it for real... or was it illusion? Typically, Axl hinted at the former...

Meanwhile, as 'Use Your Illusion' continued to ride the world's charts, reaching new peaks of precious metal as the band passed by, Singapore banned 'II' for containing "objectionable themes and profane lyrics". Curiously, the sister volume passed the censors - another bizarre footnote to the most remarkable story in modern rock which has yet to show signs of ending.

For now, though, the last word must go to Slash. "Reality for me," he explained in 1992, "is what we do as musicians, on stage, in the studio, trying to keep in control, getting on stage. Everything else is just in the way..."

22

Guns N' Roses speak their minds on:

Guns N' Roses...

Slash, Smash Hits, '88

"There's always a lot of tension going down between us. There's always something happening, sparks flying."

Slash, Music Connection, '86

"Axl is just another version of the Ayatollah."

Slash, Smash Hits, '88

". . . All of us commuted to L.A. at different times. But we were like the only guys who were as hard core as we are and doing the same kind of thing. It just kind of happened, you know."

Axl, Circus, '89

"My favorite cartoon characters are Metallica and Slash."

Axl, introducing Slash at a gig; (quoted from Smash Hits, '89)

"In a world he did not create, he will go through it as if it were his own making; half man, half beast, I don't know what it is, but it's weird and it's pissed off and it calls itself Slash!"

"Izzy sits in the corner and plays his guitar. He's very sarcastic."

Slash, Circus, '89

"Axl isn't really 24; he's a million years old – he's seen everything."

Izzy, Music Connection, '86

"We do have a fuck you attitude . . . But we know our limits. If somebody is doing something that begins to hurt the music the rest of us get down on him and say, 'You can't do that.' We're as hardcore with each other as we are with other people, and we use that hardcore attitude to keep ourselves in line."

Axl, Hit Parade, '87

Steve: "I want peace of mind."
Axl: "He really needs peace of mind 'cause when he was young, he had to go to the hospital and they took a piece of it."

From an interview in Music Connection, '86

ACCESS
ALL AREAS
IS ONLY UP TO
AND INCLUDING
ARTISTES SET

Guns N' Roses speak their minds on:

Personal Peeves...

Slash, Smash Hits, '88

"We really hate Poison – they totally emphasize everything we hate in a band! They're like the type of guys who got turned onto rock 'n' roll by Circus magazine, you know? They saw pictures and said, 'Oh yeah, this looks cool, we can get girls!' They probably went shopping and picked all their clothes and stuff and then went and bought their instruments. They pick up a guitar and learn how to play three chords and go onstage."

Axl, Metallix, '89

"It's like Slash says, a lot of these bands go out and buy their clothes and then they figure out how to play."

Axl, (referring to the song 'Out Ta Get Me'), press release, '87

"Like every time you turn around, someone is trying to screw you over financially, or the cops are banging on your door and you didn't do anything. It's just being railroaded into something and trying to get out from underneath it. You know, parents, teachers, preachers . . . everybody. The last verse Slash and I put together as a joke 'cause we were talking about how we get in fights sometimes, and how some people get pissed off that you're drunk. But they're the ones that bought the bottle of whiskey to get you drunk on. Some people say I got a chip on my shoulder."

Axl, Circus, '89

"Everyone wants to be your best friend. You get rid of them . . . you shake hands and be nice, but you know what's going on."

Axl, press release, '88

"Ever been unjustly hassled by someone with a gun and a badge? Maybe you've been conned or had someone attempt to sell you stolen property and they just won't take no for an answer. Been to a gas station or convenience store and treated like you don't belong here by an individual who can barely speak English? Hopefully not, but have you ever been attacked by a homosexual? Had some so-called religionist try to con you out of your hard-earned cash? Have you ever been banned or censored by a relatively small group of people claiming to be a majority with self-righteous and dangerous motives? This song ('One In A Million') is very simple and extremely generic or generalized, my apologies to those who may take offence."

Guns N' Roses speak their minds on:

Controversy, tittle-tattle and the sour grapes of wrath...

Slash, press release, '87

"It's kind of hard to explain this so people understand it. We were one of the most opposed bands. We had opposition from everywhere, the whole fucking time. Still, it's not as bad now 'cause we're signed and some people like the shit we do. But we started out with so many people from so many directions, trying to lash out at us. And trying to say Guns N' Roses this and that, and don't let them in here, and don't let them do this, and don't let them do that, and watch them, and this and that and the other."

Axl, Hit Parade, '87

"You know, we don't just do things to piss people off. We just do what we feel like because we don't care. We all dig playing, we're all into being musicians and we figure on doing this for as long as we can. That's really important, that it's on our terms."

Slash, Smash Hits, '88

"I was supposedly this bisexual heroin addict who had AIDS and was into small animals."

Slash, Smash Hits, '88

"You know a lot of people have a problem with us, but it's 'cause they're jealous of us. We play harder and better than most. We don't hide behind props or anything."

"We're totally anti-social and rebellious as far as the Establishment goes. The more people get bent out of shape at us and the things we do, the more we just laugh. Like, the cover of the album was going to be a picture of a naked girl and people were freaking out and getting all upset . . . We ended up using a different cover – a really cool painting – just so we could sell more records. The picture is on the inside of the record anyway."

Slash, Smash Hits, '88

"There are all these rumours that I died in a car crash and Axl and Steve O.D.'d . . ."

Slash, Hit Parade, '87

" . . . we were headed to a Roxy show and got pulled over by four cops. They picked a bag off the street; said we threw it out the window and there were drugs in it. There were no drugs in it. And they were just trying to hassle us, saying our advance money in our pockets was drug money. They searched everything, pushed us around, and we were late for the show."

Axl, press release, '87

" . . . we've learned some self control. We're not smashing interviewers' tape recorders anymore."

Slash, Metal Edge, '88

WAR? WAR?
WAR? WAR?
WAR? WAR?
WAR? WAR?
WAR? WAR?
WAR? WAR?

Guns N' Roses speak their minds on:

The days of Guns N' Roses . . .

"The band's so involving. It takes up all your time. When we're not playing, we're at a bar or a party or somewhere. We're on such a short fuse, it's tough to say what we're going to be doing at any moment."

Slash, Smash Hits, '88

"If someone puts a tape on in the bus we all try to find something good in it, even if we don't like the music. You know, anything from a cool lyric to a drum break."

Slash, Metallix, #4

"There's only so many ways you can move your hips."

Axl, Heavy Metal Sex Stars, '89

"There was all this hype about how we weren't gonna last. Those people are all eating crow now."

Duff, Circus, '89

"When we get up in the afternoon to do a soundcheck, we drink so much that we can't play, because our hands are shaking like windmills. So what happens? We drink! We drink more and more, and then we're fine, and we wake up the next day with some floosie . . . you don't know her name . . . you've got fucking weird shit on your dick . . . your bed's all wet from pissing in it, and you go, listen, will you do me a favor and find me some booze and some pizza."

Slash, Time Out, '87

"We're the kind of band we liked when we were kids, definitely a people's band."

Slash, Metal Edge, '87

" . . . Every single gig, no matter how small, is different. It's not like we're so set and we're going through the motions. Every show is something different . . . The other night I went onstage and I finished half the song before I realized I didn't have my guitar plugged in."

Slash, Stryper, '88

"It's like a melting pot. L.A. . . . This place was supposed to eat us up. All it did was make us meaner."

Axl, Concert Shots, '87

A lot of bands, especially nowadays, work too hard at creating an image too distant from the people who listen to them. They start to look so plastic and unreal that the fans think they couldn't actually get close to these people that they're listening to . . . we are more accessible – we're there for the people that are there for us."

Slash, Hit Parader, '89

Slash, Stryper, '88

"We're not really that sleazy . . . we just look that way when people compare us to a lot of other bands . . . If you compare us to a bunch of posers like some of the bands in L.A., then we come across real street and real sleazy. Let's face it, a lot of what we do stems from sexual repression in our childhood. We're just letting all the stuff we've had stored up over the years out at the same time."

Slash, Hit Parader, '89

"Hey, we don't work at the image, it's just us being us. If we wanted to change directions a little, we've already shown we're not scared to do that. What's our musical style? We don't really have any. We're just a pretty good rock and roll band."

Slash, Metallix, #4

"We're just trying to maintain a certain sanity level. Stress levels go up, stress levels go down. It's no big deal. Things keep going; doesn't stop. It's nice."

Slash, Circus, '89

"We were sort of a sore thumb on the glam scene."

Axl, Heavy Metal Sex Stars, '89

" . . . In the beginning we'd throw parties and ransack the girl's purse while one of the guys was with her."

Izzy, Music Connection, '86

"We had to eat shit to get where we are."

Guns N' Roses speak their minds on:

The biz...

Izzy, Sounds, '87

"We didn't go out and look for a record contract. It came around to us. We signed with Geffen because they were the coolest company."

Slash, Smash Hits, '88

". . . it's kind of amazing to me how people look at a record company like this huge conglomerate. When you don't have any knowledge about it, it's just this huge, mythical thing. But then you get involved in it and you realize that it's just people, and they're doing their jobs. Some of those people know their jobs and do it really well and some of those people don't do it very well. Sometimes, they have a good creative idea. Other times, they'll say, 'Well I got a deadline and I gotta make some money and I gotta get this out for my boss so I'm gonna do this my way' and it gets done that way. Also, it's a very small world, the music industry. Like people get so impressed because you write for a rock magazine and they say, 'How the fuck did they do that, man? That's incredible!' I tell 'em, 'No. It's a fuckin' job, man'!"

Guns N' Roses speak their minds on:

Hobbies, sports, etc...

Duff, Metallix, '89

"I'd just like to say that I have a personal disgust for small dogs, like poodles. I have some serious physical problems with them. Everything about them means I must kill them. I must!"

Axl (his first words to journalist Simon Garfield), Time Out, '87

"Hey, this is pretty beat. What do you say we clear off one of these tables and throw it through one of those windows?"

"I drink a lot, I collect snakes."

Axl, Heavy Metal Sex Stars, '89

"Hey, are you here on an expense account? Come on, buy us some drinks and charge it to the magazine!"

Slash, Smash Hits, '88

"If I really want it and I think there's some risk, it's Captain Trojan all the way."

Slash, Metallix, '88

"Not being sexist or anything, it's fucking amazing how much abuse girls will take."

Axl, Circus, '89

"And we don't share girlfriends."

Slash, Sounds, '87

Guns N' Roses speak their minds on:

On Gun music...

Axl, Music Connection, '86

"We just play good, straight American rock and roll, you know . . . I don't want that to sound too clichéd or anything. We play with a punch, with an edge to it."

Slash, Smash Hits, '88

"We don't want to sound just like everybody else, we don't want to mimic what people say and play – you can just take it for what it's worth. We don't take orders or crap from anybody!"

Slash, Smash Hits, '88

"Rock and roll is supposed to be a rebellion for kids, not a huge corporation. In the '60's it was the Rolling Stones, in the '70's it was Aerosmith and in the '80's it's Guns N' Roses."

Axl, Metallix, #4

"Sometimes I write some great words . . . then hear this fabulous music in my head . . . I think, 'Wow! . . . This is better than Led Zeppelin!' . . . then I go home, put on a record and I realise, shit, it was Led Zeppelin."

Axl, Time Out, '87

"I think we've come up with a sound that's pretty interesting. It's got some elements that people can recognize, but we're not ripping anyone off. Our goal is to break down as many barriers as we can. By that I mean we want to break down musical barriers by coming up with something really different, but we also want to break down some of the carriers that have popped up in people's minds. Lots of people don't want to deal with something that challenges their notion of what good music is. But we want them to do that."

Axl, Hit Parader, '88

"I know this girl named Michelle and she became a really good friend of the band's and I was going out with her for a while (Axl is referring to the inspiration of 'My Michelle'). It's a true story. Slash and some other members of the band said that's kinda too heavy to say about poor, sweet Michelle; she'll freak out. I'd written this nice sweet song about her, and then I looked at it and thought, 'that really doesn't touch any basis of reality,' so I put down an honest thing. It describes her life. This girl leads such a crazy life with doing drugs, or whatever she's doing at the time, you don't know if she's gonna be there tomorrow. Everytime I see Michelle I'm really relieved and glad. I showed her the lyrics after about three weeks of debating, and she was so happy that someone didn't paint just a pretty picture. She loves it. It was a real song about her."

Slash, Hit Parader, '89

"The nasty side of metal is what makes it appealing. There's always been that slightly dangerous side to the music, all the way back to bands like the Stones. Kids enjoy things that they know their parents don't like – something that's a little wild and crazy. That's what's made Guns N' Roses successful. But you've also got to give 'em good songs. Without that, all the outrageous things you do don't really mean sh*t."

Slash, Press Release, '87

"Have you ever found a new band and you want to turn everyone on to 'em? You want to spread the disease until you finally have 300 people hearing the same thing you hear. That's how our music spread and that's how we keep close to our roots. We're from the streets and, no matter where we go from here, we'll always have those roots."

Axl, press release, '87

"I wrote this song ('Rocket Queen') for this girl who was gonna have a band and she was gonna call it Rocket Queen. She kinda kept me alive for awhile. The last part of the song is my message to this person, or anybody else who can get something out of it. It's like there's hope and a friendship note at the end of the song. For that song there was also something I tried to work out with various people – a recorded sex act. It was somewhat spontaneous but premeditated; something I wanted to put on the record . . . It was a sexual song and it was a wild night in the studio. This girl we knew was dancing; everyone was getting really excited. The night coulda gotten really explosive, lots of trouble for everyone, and I thought wait a minute, how can we make this productive?"

Steve (referring to 'Welcome To The Jungle'), press release, '87

"I like the cowbell part."

Axl, Hit Parader, '88

"The songs are what mean the most to us . . . we all write, and we all write well. We're willing to go through hell if we can get a good song out of it . . . When I'm up onstage singing the words that capture that experience, it's all worth it."

Guns N' Roses speak their minds on:

The good old days, the bad old days, themselves, etc...

Izzy, Smash Hits, '89

"The fact that I'm from Indiana has no business being in my career!"

Axl, Concert Shots, '87

"We were a garage band back in Indiana for years, but there was no place to get gigs, unless you talked somebody into renting a hall and you'd do one gig in six months."

Steven, Smash Hits, '89

"A super bad guy just came out of me when I was a wee youngster. I was a feisty little fellow. Got thrown out of eight, nine different schools – this is just from first to third grade."

Axl, Smash Hits, '89

"When I was in school there were all these stereotypes. If you liked The Rolling Stones you were a faggot because of the time Mick Jagger kissed Keith Richards on Saturday Night Live. If you liked Grateful Dead you were a hippie. If you liked The Sex Pistols you were a punker. I guess that would make me a faggot hippie punk rocker."

Izzy, press release, '87

"It's like when you listen to a Zeppelin song, what do you think? I have all kinds of fucking wild ideas about what 'Custard Pie' is about."

Izzy, Concert Shots, '87

"Guitarists don't like showers 'cause we like the grease to build up on our fingers, makes playing more fluent!"

Slash, Metallix, #4

"Everything I own fits into two bags: One bag is full of T-shirts and the other is full of jeans. Someone stole the bag with my jeans . . . Jeans are the kind of thing where you have 'em for years and years and years 'til they get to a certain point, and someone stole eight pairs of MY jeans – every single pair of jeans I have! – and my phone book, which is like the most elaborate thing. It's like a day planner: it's got the whole album, each song, when it was recorded, basically every errand I ran over the last year, and hundreds and hundreds and hundreds of phone numbers. If you need a phone number, no matter what it is, even if it's Acme Radio Knobs Inc., I'VE got the number in my phone book. They stole that too, and my itineraries. I had a girl over one night and I wake up the next morning and she ripped off my pants and my wallet was in 'em! I had to wear a towel to a radio interview.
I didn't have anything else."

"It's weird because I've always tried not to live a structured life. Now when we tour, I have to wake up at a certain time and be somewhere by a certain time."

Axl, Metallix, #4

"We were living in the Gardener Street studio, this place where we had one little box of a room. We had no money but we could dig up a buck to go down to this liquor store. It happened to sell this great wine called Nightrain that would fuck you up for a dollar. Five dollars and you'd be gone. We lived off this stuff."

Duff, press release, '87

"Drinking hurts my throat. I'm not saying I'm anti-drinking or pro-drinking, it just dries my throat out, that's all."

Axl, Metallix, #4

"We love to take care of women – we love to treat them great – but right now we don't have any money so we treat them like shit . . ."

Izzy, Music Connection, '86

"I just don't trust chicks anymore. If they want to be with me at a show, fine. I've had it with taking girls home."

Slash, Metallix, #4

"I really like Metallica. They're like the best band doing anything in rock 'n' roll in the past ten years. They're just like the greatest. I also really like Megadeath."

Slash, Smash Hits, '88

"I mean, I'm just a kid . . . I belong out there with them, not here. It really blows me away when I think about it."

Slash, Metallix, #4

"There's a lot to say for the period of time when you start to lose the excitement of chasing chicks. You start going after really bizarre girls, like librarians and stuff. Just to catch 'em; to say I finally went out and caught a girl that wouldn't be my normal kinda date, 'cause everything else is startin' to get . . . 'it's so easy'."

Slash, press release, '87

"When I was in the first grade, I wasn't allowed to cross the street until I sang two Elvis Presley songs. And then, when I was in third grade, at recess, I would have to get up on top of a tree stump, and the teachers would make me sing all the Top-40 and Elvis tunes for the younger kids."

Axl, Concert Shots, '87

"I remember sweeping those bowling alleys and washing those dishes and making pizzas and hamburgers . . . the whole bit, I did it all."

Steven, Metallix, '89

Duff, Stryper, '88

"A lot of money would be like instant suicide. I'm scared of the responsibility of having a lot of money."

Slash, Metallix, '89

"Whenever I don't drink I get the weirdest dreams, I had this one dream that I'm doing a guest spot for Tiffany! Do you know who Tiffany is? Anyway, I walk all the way up to the stage and I'm waiting for my cue, and the whole debate of whether or not this would be cool to do or not starts. You know how dreams are – it's so real! So here I am, sitting around behind all the flight cases and stuff, waiting for my cue to go on, and I'm wondering whether I should do this thing with Tiffany. Right before it was going to happen, I woke up! They say you always wake up right before you're going to die (in dreams), right? It was funny as sh*t!"

"I had a dream that I was out in South America catching chameleons . . . I have some fuckin' weirdo dreams. I had some dreams not too long ago, the ones that are like super-super-super violent and you get into these gnarly situations? I always have my guitars stolen in my dreams. It only happens to me when I'm sober; when I'm drunk I sleep soundly. But when I'm sober I have these dreams like I can't even believe! It's to the point where I have so many bad dreams that they're not like bad dreams – they're kinda exciting!"

Slash, Metal Edge, '89

"I don't have a home. I have no place to store my shit . . . Everything I have is with me."

Steven Hit Parader, '89

"I was born a poor black child."

Slash, Hit Parader, '89

"It's a good enough compliment just for somebody to say 'Your music is great' or 'I enjoy your band'. To walk, talk and dress like me is taking it a little far."

Steven, Metallix, '88

"I just want to keep playing forever. I love playing, ya can't beat it. Out of all the crappy jobs I've had in my life, I appreciate it very much."

Slash, Circus, '89

"I am sorry to say, I don't really know how to live in any kind of stable environment."

"We didn't have any money, but we had a lot of hangers on and girls we could basically live off of . . . things were just too easy. There's an emptiness."

Izzy, (on the bad old days) press release, '87

"I'm always on the edge. It's a very, very dangerous place to be."

Axl, Circus, '89

"A lot of people hold their anger back for a few days, but I just explode right away."

Axl, Circus, April, '89

"Sometimes there's these girls backstage going 'I love you'. I feel like saying, 'Honey, if you knew me, you would hate my fuckin' guts. So why don't you just say, 'Hi. I like you. It's cool. Wanna sign an autograph?' Or they want my phone number. I should come up with some answering machine type thing and just set it up all the time in L.A. Like the Axl Hotline or something. I'd just tell girls to go buy fax machines and fax stuff out!"

Axl, Heavy Metal Sex Stars, '89

"If I had one wish, I'd ask for a constant supply of Marlboros."

Slash, Music Connection, '86

" . . . Up until we got signed, I lived on the street for five years. I never lived in one place for more than two months, always crashing at people's houses. My parents would say, 'Come back home and go to college and we'll pay for it' but I would reply, 'No, I have to do this now'."

Axl, Hit Parade, '87

"You should see this hotel room I'm living in. It's got holes in the walls . . . I'm just sick of this place. It's a damn pigsty. It's turned into a commune. Everybody comes here when they're down and out. I can't turn people away 'cause I know what it's like with no place to crash. Every single night man, this place is crowded. I can't take it, it's driving me nuts."

Slash, Metallix, #4

"Fuck you and your magazine. There'll be no shit about me being from Indiana. It deserves nothing; it was a worthless fucking city . . ."

Izzy, Music Connection, '86

s N' Roses speak their minds on: hat's on their minds . . .

Axl, Hit Parade, '87

"We want to stay one step ahead of everyone else. We know this is our big chance and we're sure not gonna blow it."

Slash, Smash Hits, '88

"If there's anything we've got to say, it's don't take anything at face value, don't listen to other people's opinions before you've reached your own conclusions – most people don't know what they're talking about. We've gotten ahead by sticking to our roots and not taking crap from anybody. That pisses people off."

Axl, Smash Hits, '89

"We're working on getting everything we want, our way – all the money, all the power, and all the control over everything there is."

Slash, Hit Parade, '87

" . . . we've got real strong ideas of our own. We will take suggestions. But the bottom line is that we'll fight real hard for what we believe in. And why not? We know we're always going to be at odds with people on something. But the bands who have made it big are the ones who have always been that way."

Izzy, Smash Hits, '89

"We don't care if people think we've got a bad attitude."

Steven, press release, '87

"Loud is a way of life."

Axl, press release, '87

"We'd rather be unknown and live in Idaho than to have someone tell us what to play and how to 'make it' . . ."

Duff, Metallix, #4

"We're really big over there (in England), we've been generating a lot of shit. Our crowds are punkers, metalers . . . You see, over there is this whole rock and roll thing, but there's no band that the kids can hang on to. There's nothing. It's funny – it's us now for those street-level kids over there, even though we're American, although I think the only reasons that they can relate more to our songs than, say, somebody else like Poison is they don't sing about real things, you know. The kids don't really have any money to piss away. Have I said something wrong? They're really repressed. They can't relate to somebody singing about 'Steal my keys to my Daddy's car/Go to the drive-in . . .' They can't relate to that at all. It's bullshit, American crap. I'm not just saying these things as my own opinion. I've been told this by English people. They can really relate to us and our music."

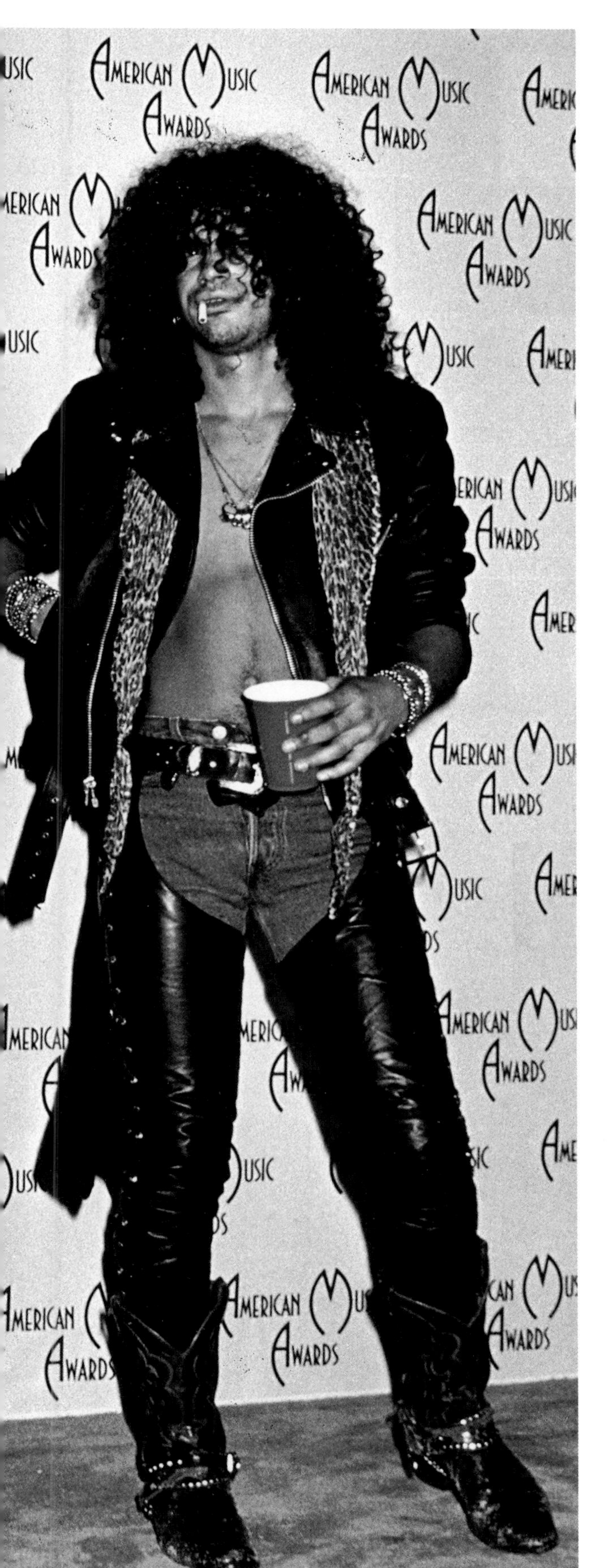

"I can't understand how some bands could deal with the mundane kind of lives they lead. The ones that go in the press, 'Oh we party and every night's this and that and doin' girls and blah-blah-blah . . .' and it's all bullshit. I can't understand how bands can be like that, how they can be so phony about the shit that they do and then live a dull existence. I just couldn't live any other way; I'd be bored out of my mind. I don't care what kind of toll it takes on me in the long run. I'd rather live fast now than live slow and die with white hair and having never done anything I ever wanted to do."

Slash, Metallix, #4

" . . . I still don't think I'm better than anybody else. Nobody's different than anybody else. Everybody eats, sleeps, drinks, shits, fucks, just like the rest of 'em. That's why I figure I got this far. Eddie Van Halen ain't no different, and if he could do it, I could do it. So I did it too."

Steven, Metallix, '89

" . . . A band can keep you together. Like we can go through all kinds of shit, but the band keeps us together. But if you don't have a band, don't have a job, then somehow drugs seem to take over . . ."

Slash, Press Release, '87

"What we're trying to do is we're trying to get people to break down their shells and be themselves."

Axl, Metallix, '89

"I know that things catch up to you. I'm not the kind of person that goes into anything except with both feet. I learn all my lessons the hard way."

Axl, Hit Parade, '87

". . . you can stay in the most expensive hotels and you can be a huge rock band and have a lot of fame and recognition and all that stuff, but when you get into the rooms, toilet paper is still toilet paper."

Slash, Hit Parader, '89

"If we have to desperately hold on to what we are, it's time to pack it in, quit and die."

Slash, Circus, '89

"We take everything – and that goes in every single way, we take everything from everything we hear, from what we see and do."

Axl, Sounds, '87

"We never set out to be role models for kids. We're just us. If some kid is dumb enough to try to act like us, we take no responsibility for what might happen. The kind of life we lead is good for us – but we've been lucky. You could end up dead just as easily as having a Number 1 album."

Duff, Hit Parader, '89

Road kill . . .

Duff, Metallix, '89

"Headlining's more fun because it's your crowd, ya know. See with the Crüe it's fun, but it's not your crowd. You're just trying to kick ass, which is another aspect of it. But this is your crowd, all those 5,500 people with their arms in the air are there for you."

Slash, Smash Hits, '88

"Basically, we're a road band, we really get off on touring."

Axl, Smash Hits, '89

"You can't sleep as late as you want."

Slash, Smash Hits, '89

"All of this is really weird when I start to think about it."

"L.A. may be great and all that but shit . . . I want to get back on the road! I can't take being in one place for too long."

Slash, Metallix, '89

"We were with Alice Cooper in the midwest. It started snowing. I hadn't seen snow in ages, since I was a little kid. I said 'Oh, snow, cool . . .' The novelty wore off real quick. Five minutes of it and I said 'Okay, that's enough!"

Slash, Hit Parade, '89

"I checked into this hotel and went to sleep. Early in the morning, I was woken up by this sound that was like someone getting hit over the head with a tire iron or something – a really sick noise . . . some guy had jumped off the roof and hit the ledge outside my room on the way down. I had the curtains pulled down . . . so I didn't look . . . but then our tour manager came knocking on my door asking if I was alright. He thought I had jumped out the window. It was really bizarre. The poor guy who had jumped was a real mess. They didn't even come to get him for four hours. The sickest part was that our tour manager, who had a room facing what went on, put up cards grading the jump like he was an Olympic diving judge."

"If we were in New York we would be out buying shit or something. This (Grand Rapids) is like other urban cities. There's nowhere to go, really, so all you can do is kill time in the hotel. You can usually go out and shop in the malls – malls are good places."

"The gigs are getting bigger now. The only big difference I notice is that when you get a gig you're sort of like flipped out because of the size of the place and then seeing all these backstage preparations going on. It's just the whole big production and preparation for you, you know? All of a sudden there's four semis out front instead of one. Like the Motley tour, it used to blow me away. All the amounts of people working, you know getting this whole thing on the road . . ."

Izzy, Metallix, '88

"The crowds have been incredible. Especially one night in Indiana – or Illinois or something. It was the best day of my life. I just tapped my bass drum, boom boom boom, and over 5,000 people all had their hands in the air. It was the best thing, the best!"

Slash, Metallix, '88

"Sometimes when we're on tour I get these huge cuts on my hands. I try putting this junk known as 'liquid skin' on those cuts, so they have a chance to heal. But it doesn't work. I just keep bleeding, and the stuff just keeps the cuts open and actually prevents them from healing. But that's part of being a drummer. I play so hard that my hands just blister. They don't heal until after we stop touring – and we haven't been off the road in a year."

Steven, Metallix, '88

"When you're headlining you have all this time to kill between dinner and when you have to play. I used to just sit around and drink, only you end up getting really drunk by the time you have to play. When you're opening up you play a couple of hours earlier and then you have the rest of the night to get drunk and mess around."

Steven, Hit Parader, '89

". . . out here in small towns, you are the focal point. Here, they just swarm around you man, like four of 'em will see you and they come over and talk to you and then eight other people see you and they come over and all of a sudden it's like this wave of people and it's kind of like, 'Whoa, I gotta get out of here man!' And they're trying to steal your rings. In the bigger cities like L.A. and New York, they're used to seeing people in bands all the time, so they don't give a shit . . . The other night me and Slash went out in the crowd, in like an alleyway for the PA guys with the crowd all around. Well, we just walked out to watch Zodiac (Mindwarp) and there was like 50 people just trying to dive over the balcony and shit to get to us! We were like, 'Uh-oh, we better get the hell out of here.' I mean, it doesn't scare me . . . it's just a pain."

Duff, Metallix, '88

Guns N' Roses speak their minds on:

The look you may (or may not) want to know

Slash, Smash Hits, '88

"We don't put much time into preparing for a show or anything. We just go out there wearing whatever we've got on and get on with it. That's what everybody wants to see anyway."

Axl, Hit Parader, '89

"I used to fluff up my hair and tease it out, but I don't really do it anymore. It's not that I don't like it but I don't do it well unless I take a long time at it and I don't bring someone on the road with me to do it. Also, after our falling out with Poison – even though it's been patched up – I just want to get away from anything glam until such a time that I can go out and do it if I want to and not get hassled. It's not so much that I'm worried about what other people think, but I know me. If someone walks up to me and says, 'Oh, you're a glam faggot like Poison,' I'm gonna go to jail, 'cause I'm gonna break somebody's jaw."

Steve, Concert Shots, '87

"The image is a non-image."

Axl, Hit Parader, '87

"When I came to L.A. five years ago from some hellhole in the Midwest, I was wearing cowboy boots and everyone said I looked like I just came off the boat. All of a sudden, it's become a fashion, so now I guess I drive the boat."

U.K. LPs

APPETITE FOR DESTRUCTION
Geffen WX125 (August 1987)

APPETITE FOR DESTRUCTION
Geffen WX125W (1988, Limited w/stickers)

G 'N' R LIES
Geffen WX218 (December 1988)

G 'N' LIES
Geffen WX218W (1988, Limited w/stickers)

USE YOUR ILLUSION I
Geffen GEF 24415 (September 1991)

USE YOUR ILLUSION II
Geffen GEF 24420 (September 1991)

U.K. CDs

APPETITE FOR DESTRUCTION
Geffen 9241482 (1987)

G 'N' R LIES
Geffen 9241982 (1988)

GUNS N'ROSES
Baktabak CBAK4015
(November 1989, interview compact disc)

USE YOUR ILLUSION I
Geffen GEFC 24415 (September 1991)

USE YOUR ILLUSION II
Geffen GEFC 24420 (September 1991)

U.K. SPECIAL

SWEET CHILD OF MINE/OUT TA GET ME/ ROCKET QUEEN
Geffen GEF 43TE (August 1988, special sleeve, 10")

WELCOME TO THE JUNGLE/NIGHTRAIN/ YOU'RE CRAZY
Geffen GEF 47CD (October 1988, CD Single)

PARADISE CITY/I USED TO LOVE HER/ ANYTHING GOES
Geffen GEF 50CD (March 1989, CD Single)

PARADISE CITY/I USED TO LOVE HER/ SWEET CHILD OF MINE
Geffen 9275704 (March 1989, cassette single)

PARADISE CITY/I USED TO LOVE HER
Geffen GEF 50P
(March 1989, pic. disc. single; gun shaped)

PARADISE CITY/I USED TO LOVE HER
Geffen GEF50X (March 1989, holster package)

GUNS N'ROSES INTERVIEW PICTURE DISC
Music & Media CT1013 (December 1987)

GUNS N'ROSES INTERVIEW PICTURE DISC
Baktabak BAK2079 (December 1987)

GUNS N'ROSES INTERVIEW PICTURE DISC COLLECTION
Baktabak BAKPAK1011 (1988, 7" Set)

APPETITE FOR CONVERSATION
Baktabak BAK6001
(March 1989, interview picture disc LP)

U.K. SINGLES

IT'S SO EASY/MR. BROWNSTONE
Geffen GEF22 (June 1987)

WELCOME TO THE JUNGLE/ WHOLE LOTTA ROSIE
Geffen GEF30 (September 1987)

WELCOME TO THE JUNGLE/NIGHTRAIN
Geffen GEF47 (October 1988)

PARADISE CITY/I USED TO LOVE HER
Geffen GEF50 (March 1989)

PATIENCE/ROCKET QUEEN
Geffen GEF56 (May 1989)

SWEET CHILD O'MINE/OUT TO GET ME
Geffen GEF43 (August 1988)

SWEET CHILD O'MINE/ OUT TO GET ME (Re-release)
Geffen GEF55 (May 1989)

NIGHTRAIN/RECKLESS LIFE
Geffen GEF60 (August 1989)

YOU COULD BE MINE/CIVIL WAR
Geffen GFS6 (July 1991)

DON'T CRY/DON'T CRY (Alternate lyrics)
Geffen GFS9 (August 1991)

LIVE AND LET DIE/LIVE AND LET DIE (Live)
Geffen GFS17 (December 1991)

NOVEMBER RAIN/SWEET CHILD O'MINE
Geffen GFS18 (February 1992)

Double A-side
KNOCKIN' ON HEAVEN'S DOOR (LP Version)/
KNOCKIN' ON HEAVEN'S DOOR
(Live at Wembley, 20 April 1992)
Geffen GFS21 (May 1992)

IT'S SO EASY/MR. BROWNSTONE/
SHADOW OF YOUR LOVE/ MOVE TO THE CITY
Geffen GEF 22T (June 1987)

IT'S SO EASY/MR. BROWNSTONE/
SHADOW OF YOUR LOVE/ MOVE TO THE CITY
Geffen GEF 22TP (June 1987, pic. disc)

WELCOME TO THE JUNGLE/
WHOLE LOTTA ROSIE/IT'S SO EASY/
KNOCKIN' ON HEAVEN'S DOOR
Geffen GEF 30T (September 1987)

WELCOME TO THE JUNGLE/
WHOLE LOTTA ROSIE/IT'S SO EASY/
KNOCKIN' ON HEAVEN'S DOOR
Geffen GEF 30TW
(September 1987, w/poster sleeve)

WELCOME TO THE JUNGLE/
WHOLE LOTTA ROSIE/IT'S SO EASY/
KNOCKIN' ON HEAVEN'S DOOR
Geffen GEF 30TP (September 1987, pic. disc)

SWEET CHILD OF MINE/OUT TA GET ME/
ROCKET QUEEN
Geffen GEF 43T (August 1988)

SWEET CHILD OF MINE/OUT TA GET ME/
ROCKET QUEEN
Geffen GEF 43TV (August 1988 in special sleeve)

WELCOME TO THE JUNGLE/NIGHTRAIN/
YOU'RE CRAZY
Geffen GEF 47T (October 1988)

WELCOME TO THE JUNGLE/NIGHTRAIN/
YOU'RE CRAZY
Geffen GEF 47TW (October 1988, poster sleeve)

WELCOME TO THE JUNGLE/NIGHTRAIN/
YOU'RE CRAZY
Geffen GEF 47TV (October 1988, w/patch)

WELCOME TO THE JUNGLE/NIGHTRAIN/
YOU'RE CRAZY
Geffen GEF 47TP (October 1988, pic. disc)

PARADISE CITY/I USED TO LOVE HER/
ANYTHING GOES
Geffen GEF 50T (March 1989)

PATIENCE/ROCKET QUEEN/
W.AXL.ROSE INTERVIEW
Geffen GEF 56T (May 1989)

NIGHTRAIN/RECKLESS LIFE/
KNOCKIN' ON HEAVEN'S DOOR (Live)
Geffen GEF60T (August 1989)

YOU COULD BE MINE/CIVIL WAR
Geffen GFST 6 (July 1991)

DON'T CRY/DON'T CRY (Alternate lyrics)/
DON'T CRY (Demo)
Geffen GFST 9 (August 1991)

LIVE AND LET DIE/LIVE AND LET DIE (Live)
Geffen GFST 17 (December 1991)

NOVEMBER RAIN/SWEET CHILD O'MINE/
PATIENCE
Geffen GFST 18 (February 1992)

KNOCKIN' ON HEAVEN'S DOOR (LP Version)/
KNOCKIN' ON HEAVEN'S DOOR
(Live at Wembley, 20 April 1992)
Geffen GFST (May 1992)

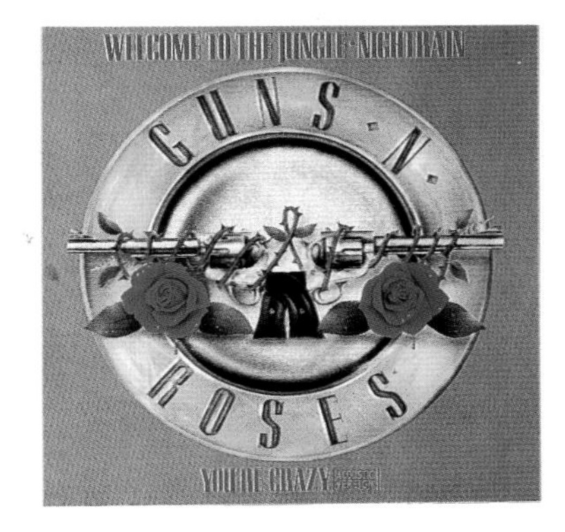

4/93 (15394)

SES
LES